China 2030

Angang Hu • Yilong Yan • Xing Wei

China 2030

 Springer

Angang Hu
Center for China Studies
School of Public Policy and Management
Tsinghua University
Beijing, China

Yilong Yan
Institute of Education and Researcher
Institute for Contemporary China Studies
Tsinghua University
Beijing, China

Xing Wei
School of Public Policy and Management
Tsinghua University
Beijing, China

ISBN 978-3-662-51034-6   ISBN 978-3-642-31328-8 (eBook)
DOI 10.1007/978-3-642-31328-8
Springer Heidelberg New York Dordrecht London

Printed on acid-free paper

Springer is part of Springer Science+Business Media (www.springer.com)

Contents

Chapter 1
Brief Introduction

A great nation has a great dream; a great country has a great dream. China's dream is to build a society of common prosperity and a world in which all people live together in peace and harmony. China did not begin its journey toward this great dream until after the founding of the New China, more so after its reform and opening up. The Chinese people will come close to realizing this great dream by 2030.

This book provides predictions up to 2030 regarding the future major developments and trends of both China and the world in general from a historical and worldwide perspective. It analyzes the impact of interactions between China and the rest of the world using a strategic view and a specialized study of national and international conditions. By carrying forward the spirit of Chinese culture and spreading the socialist theory of common prosperity, this book spells out the dreams of all mankind in the pursuit of common prosperity. It also offers China's vision and perspective to the world, as well as Chinese scholars' perspective on and worldwide vision for the future.

The year 2030 will see China become a country with a population of more than a billion people, sharing prosperity, national power and a beautiful homeland. China will become a world economic power in the real sense of the term, with a GDP aggregate 2.0–2.2 times that of the United States, and its human development index 3.2 times greater. It will become a green homeland, with blue skies, clear water and beautiful landscapes.

The year 2030 will witness more than 200 countries and regions, and more than 8 billion people embark on a road to universal harmony. The whole world will experience unprecedented development; the south and the north will experience unprecedented convergence and the north–south divide will undergo an exceptional reversal, further influencing the shift in the main development indicators, which have gone from 30:70 (20–30 years ago) to 50:50 (present day), and are predicted to be at 70:30 (in another 20–30 years).

As predicted by Mao Zedong, "Peace would then reign over the world, with all people under heaven to share the same warmth and cold."

A. Hu et al., *China 2030*, DOI 10.1007/978-3-642-31328-8_1,
© Springer-Verlag Berlin Heidelberg 2014

Chapter 2
China's Dream and Roadmap

Fraternity, equality and justice
– This is a world of great universal harmony.

Kang Youwei (1913)

Fifty years ago, Comrade Mao Zedong pointed out prophetically, "The next fifty (2012) or hundred years (2062) from now will be an epic period of fundamental change in the social system of the world, an earth-shaking period, with which no past era can be compared.... Living in such a period, we must be prepared to carry out great struggles, differing in many respects from the forms of struggle of previous periods" (Mao Zedong 1999a). Three earth-shattering events then took place in China in the latter half of the twentieth century and these changes exceeded any previous historical events. The first significant event was the founding of a New China. The Chinese people stood up and a socialist system was established, with the people becoming the masters of their country for the first time in history. The second major event was the establishment of an independent and complete industrial system and a national economic system in 1949–1978. This paved the way institutionally, in human resources and industries, for the subsequent reform and opening up of China. The third major event was the reform and opening up after 1978, which fully realized China's productivity, offering China's people a better standard of living.

Likewise, further earth-shattering changes will occur in the first half of the twenty-first century. China will accomplish a further three major undertakings that will enable the country to realize full modernization by the middle of the century. It will become a wealthy, strong, democratic-socialist country with a high level of civility, and will go on to create new miracles. The first major undertaking is to build a comprehensive and prosperous society in the first 20 years of this century. The second is to construct a society with common prosperity by 2030. This stage is a developmental one that will build the foundations of the third stage. It is the inevitable extension of a prosperous society and also an inevitable path to complete modernization. The third undertaking is to realize complete socialist modernization.

A. Hu et al., *China 2030*, DOI 10.1007/978-3-642-31328-8_2,
© Springer-Verlag Berlin Heidelberg 2014

The world will also undergo tremendous changes in the following decades. Great development will occur as the world holds its largest ever population and engages in a multitude of economic activities. These factors will reverse the current unequal structure of international players and the global order dominated by just a few Western powers. For the first time in human history, there will appear a scene of common development, common prosperity and common progress among the more than eight billion citizens of the world. The remarkable changes that will take place in China are bound to trigger further significant changes worldwide, which will, in turn, stimulate and promote changes in China. The general orientation of these changes will be toward a harmonious world.

China's Dream: Common Prosperity and a Harmonious World

Great nations and countries need great dreams. Each nation and country has different dreams during different eras. China and its people have always had a great dream and have been pursuing it constantly to realize its fulfillment.

More than 2000 years ago, Confucius visualized a dream for China of "great harmony" and a "prosperous society". He perceived an ideal society as being:

> When the perfect order prevails, the world is like a home shared by all. Virtuous and worthy men are elected to public office, and capable men hold posts of gainful employment in society; peace and trust among all men are the maxims of living. All men love and respect their own parents and children, as well as the parents and children of others. There is caring for the old; there are jobs for the adults; there are nourishment and education for children. There is a means of support of widows, and the widowers; for all who find themselves alone in the world; and for the disabled. Every man and woman has an appropriate role to play in the family and society. A sense of sharing displaces the effects of selfishness and materialism. A devotion to public duty leaves no room for idleness. Intrigues and conniving for ill gain are unknown. Villains such as thieves and robbers do not exist. The door to every home need never be locked and bolted by day or night. These are the characteristics of an ideal world, a world of great harmony.[1]

Confucius viewed a harmonious world as a "utopia." The real world has to be a "prosperous" society, just short of a world of great harmony.

Despite the fact that throughout history China has been carved up by various Western powers and has experienced significant decline, the Chinese people have never given up their pursuit of their great dream. Kang Youwei reaffirmed and further developed the age-old dream of "great harmony" when he said that developed capitalism was not the ultimate goal of humanity, but was rather a stage closer to peace, which is then followed by a higher stage of social development; that is, a world of great harmony is one where all boundaries and differences are eliminated (including the nine boundaries between states, classes, races, gender, families, property, animals and man, professions, rural and urban areas, and mountainous

---

[1] "Book of Sites: Li Yun".

and plains, as well as sufferings.) and all men are equal and all people in the world enjoy happiness.[2]

In 1905, Dr. SunYat-sen stated that China would overtake the West.[3] In 1924, he made his famous speech "The Three Principles of the People", stating that the real principles of the people (the Principles of Nationalism, Principles of Democracy and Principles of People's Livelihood) are the principles of the world of great harmony that Confucius longed for. The future society he was striving for is a society in which there would be no disparity between rich and poor, neither would there be injustice (where a minority rich oppresses the poor). It is a society in which "all people live equally a happy life, totally realizing a society of the people, by the people and for the people, truly realizing what the ancients dreamed of – a world of great harmony." (Sun Wen 1924)

However, the ideal worlds envisaged by Confucius, Kang Youwei, and Dr. Sun Yat-sen are nothing but utopias. These men did not and could not possibly find the path to great harmony. In the past, foreign countries enjoyed bourgeois republics but China could not because it was a country subject to imperialist oppression. The only way out for China was to establish a people's republic under the leadership of the working class (Mao Zedong 1991). This was the historical conclusion arrived at by Mao Zedong on the eve of the founding of the New China in 1949, when he had no more time to formulate a dream state for contemporary China.

After the founding of the New China, the people were liberated and the country achieved national independence, abolished the system of exploitation, and founded the new socialist system. This was the institutional basis for China, and one-fifth of the world's population, to start pursuing and realizing a "world of great harmony". It was the first time that China's far-fetched dream appeared to be possible.

What was Mao Zedong's dream for China? It was a strong socialist country with common prosperity. In December 1955, he said

> Our goal is to make China much developed, much wealthier and much stronger than at present. Now, our country is neither wealthy nor strong. It is a very poor country.… We have practiced this kind of system (socialist system), such a plan (the first five-year plan), which will make us wealthier and stronger year by year and we may see the country growing wealthier and stronger year by year. But this wealth is common wealth and the strength is common strength … we are all sure of such common prosperity, not without knowing what to do tomorrow (Mao Zedong 1999b).

His words contain three meanings. One is that China must change its status from a weak country to a strong country; another is that the Chinese people must shake off poverty and embark on a road to common prosperity; and lastly that China must remain on the socialist road so as to ensure common prosperity for the people, who will share the benefits of a strong China. Mao Zedong maintained his

---

[2] For details, see Kang Youwei (1994).

[3] See "Min Bao", No. 1, quoting late Premier Zhou Enlai's "Government Work Report", December 21–22, 1964. See the CPC Central Documentation Office: *Selected Important Documents since the Founding of New China*, Vol. 19, P. 492, Beijing, Central Documentation Press.

belief in socialist equity his entire life and was dedicated to the goal of reducing the differences between industry and agriculture, urban and rural, and manual and mental labor, through the elimination of exploitation.

Although Mao Zedong failed to rid the country of poverty, let alone reach the desired levels of common prosperity, through a generation's tireless efforts China has attained a relatively high level of human development from a low level of income, and has built an equitable socialist society.[4] This work prepared the material, social and fundamental political system bases for China's reform and opening up, and ensured that China continued along the socialist road toward common prosperity.

After 1979, Deng Xiaoping continued China's dream of building a well-off society. He said that the goals of "well-off" families,[5] "well-off" levels (Deng Xiaoping 1994b), and a "well-off" society[6] would maintain China's historical ideal of "great harmony" and represent an ideal contemporary China. These notions are different from the traditional sense of "well-off". Furthermore, they reflect the socialist ideal and orientation for common prosperity. He clearly pointed out; "The greatest superiority of socialism is that it enables all the people to prosper, and common prosperity is the essence of socialism (Deng Xiaoping 1993b)." He proposed a roadmap toward common prosperity known as the "two-step" theory. The first step is to enable some to "get rich first,"; the second step is common prosperity, with those who became wealthy first to include those who did not, and to achieve common prosperity for all.[7] Thus, China's development has been divided into two stages: the first stage,

---

[4] The World Bank stated in its China Study Report at the beginning of the 1980s that China's development strategy and the current system have on the whole created an extremely equal society. The inequality in urban income was very low and there was no extreme poverty in Chinese cities. In the first decade after the revolution, the country adopted measures to greatly reduce the inequality and poverty in rural areas. In the ensuing 20 years, rural income distribution may be more unequal (World Bank Economic Study Tour 1983).

[5] On December 6, 1979, Deng Xiaoping said during his talk with Masayoshi Ohira, Prime Minister of Japan, "The four modernizations we are striving to achieve are modernizations with Chinese characteristics. Our concept of the four modernizations is different from yours. By achieving the four modernizations, we mean achieving a comparative prosperity. Even if we realize the four modernizations by the end of this century, our per capita GNP will still be very low. If we want to reach the level of a relatively wealthy country of the Third World with a per capita GNP US $1,000 for example…. However, at that point China will be a country with a comparative prosperity" (Deng Xiaoping 1994a).

[6] March 25, 1984, Deng Xiaoping said during his meeting with the Japanese Prime Minister Yasuhiro Nakasone "If, by the end of the century, the annual gross value of industrial and agricultural output is quadrupled, and the average per capita GNP reaches US$800, then we shall have a society in which people lead a fairly comfortable life. Realizing this society is what we call Chinese-style modernization. Quadrupling production, attaining a fairly comfortable level of life and Chinese-style modernization are all new concepts we have formed" (Deng Xiaoping 1993a).

[7] Deng Xiaoping said, "The purpose of allowing some regions and some people to become prosperous before others is to enable all of them to prosper eventually. We have to make sure that there is no polarization of society—that's what socialism means" (Deng Xiaoping 1993c).

1978–2001, featured the "get rich first" theory, and the second stage after 2002, largely represents the "common prosperity" theory.[8]

In April 1987, Deng Xiaoping expounded, for the first time, a complete three-stage strategy. The first step was to double per capita GNP, reaching US$500 in the 1980s (at US$250, the 1980 per capita GNP was used as the base figure). The second step was to further double per capita GNP to US$1,000 by the end of the twentieth century. The realization of the goal would represent a "well-off" society, turning poverty-stricken China into a "well-off" nation, when GNP would top US$1 trillion. Although China's per capita GNP is still very low, the strength of the country as a whole has grown. The third step of Deng Xiaoping's long-term development, the most important step, was to quadruple China's per capita income to US$4,000 in 30–50 years time (in the first half of the twenty-first century) (Deng Xiaoping 1993d).

Deng Xiaoping pointed out that the essence of socialism is common prosperity, which has two important hallmarks and objectives: the first is prosperity levels, with per capita GNP reaching US$4,000 (at 1980s values), equal to that of mid-level developed countries; the second is common prosperity. Deng Xiaoping stated, "When we succeed in raising China's per capita GNP to US$4,000 and everyone is prosperous, that will better demonstrate the superiority of socialism over capitalism, it will chart the course for three quarters of the world's population, and it will provide further proof of the correctness of Marxism" (Deng Xiaoping 1993c).

In 2002, Jiang Zemin described in his report to the 16th National Party Congress a grand goal for China: he hoped for a more prosperous society by 2020, one that would benefit China's population of more than one billion people. He set goals to quadruple China's 2000 GDP levels by 2020 and the realization of industrialization (Jiang Zemin 2005). His aim was to have per capita GDP at more than US$3,000 by 2020, equal to that of middle-income countries, with an urbanization rate of more than 50%, and agricultural rates reduced to 30% (Zeng Peiyan 2009).

In 2007, in his report to the 17th National Party Congress, President Hu Jintao introduced a new demand for a prosperous society by 2020. He presented a clearer and more complete blueprint for 2020[9] and set higher objectives: the 2000 level of

---

[8] The author gave a comment on the report to the 16th Party Congress during an interview in the Focus slot of CCTV on the evening of October 15, 2002: "Over the past 20 years, the main theme of development is to let some of the people get prosperous and let some of the regions prosper first". Over the next 20 years, the main theme will be the building of a "well-off society", which will enable all people to move toward common prosperity. For details, See: Angang Hu (2002).

[9] Hu Jintao said "When the goal of building a well-off society in all respects is attained by 2020, China, a large developing socialist country with an ancient civilization, will have basically accomplished industrialization, with its overall strength significantly increased and its domestic market ranking as one of the largest in the world. It will be a country whose people are better off and enjoy markedly improved quality of life and a good environment. Its citizens will have more extensive democratic rights, show higher ethical standards and look forward to greater cultural achievements. China will have better institutions in all areas and Chinese society will have greater vitality coupled with stability and unity. The country will be still more open and friendly to the outside world and make greater contributions to human civilization" (Hu Jintao 2007).

per capita GDP was to quadruple by 2020 to reach 40,000 yuan or US$5,000, the urbanization rate will be close to 60% (Lin Zhaomu 2007), and the percentage of middle-income earners should increase from 15–20% to 50% (Liu He 2007), with everyone enjoying minimum living costs and elementary health services.

The goal of building a prosperous society is integration of the aims of socialist modernization and traditional ideals regarding prosperity. China has already accomplished ahead of time Deng Xiaoping's two-step strategy, as per capita GDP reached 5,980 yuan in 2010 (calculated using the 1980 fixed price). We have also realized 40 years ahead of time the strategic conception of Deng Xiaoping's third development step, as per capita GNP has already reached US$4,000.

Thus, China has by and large realized its objective to quadruple GDP by 2015 and is 5 years ahead of time for the goal put forward by the 16th National Party Congress. If we also realize the goal to quadruple per capita GDP again by 2017, China will have achieved the objective put forward at the 17th National Party Congress. If the urbanization rate reaches 50% in 2011, we will have accomplished 9 years ahead of time the task put forward at the 16th National Party Congress. The urbanization rate is expected to reach 60% by 2018, fulfilling the objective put forward by the 17th National Party Congress 2 years ahead of time.

Despite these achievements, we have not attained the goal of common prosperity, the second goal put forward by Deng Xiaoping. There are still many outstanding problems including income disparity and social inequality despite incomes increasing across the board.

It is, therefore, necessary to put forward a long-term strategic and forward-looking development goal for 2030. Thus, China's significant population needs to work together to construct a socialist China with common prosperity. This is both a natural extension of the goal to build a prosperous society in its real sense and a historical necessity, and a transit station on the inevitable path toward socialist modernization by 2050. In the following two decades, China will transition from a prosperous society to a wealthy society, from a population of lower-middle income earners to high-income earners. Common prosperity is the key development theme for socialist China; it is the central development goal and the most significant development task. Common prosperity is the crystallization of the organic integration of China's socialist modernization and the notion of building a world of great harmony.

Thirty years ago Deng Xiaoping commented "The Chinese people will, through their own creative labor, fundamentally change where they feel lagging behind and stand aloft among the advanced ranks of the world with a brand new outlook and will, together with the people of other countries, push the just cause of humankind."[10]

---

[10] This is a foreword written by Deng Xiaoping on February 14, 1981 for the book *Speeches and writings: Deng Xiaoping* published by Pergamon Press Ltd. CPC Central Documentation Office, *Chronicle of Deng Xiaoping* (1975–1997) Vol. II, pp. 713–714, Beijing, Central Documentation Press, 2004.

The just cause he refers to is common development, common prosperity, and common wealth. This is the source and basis of our creation.

Chinese society in 2030 will hopefully represent a common wealth society and a world of great harmony. It encompasses the three points described below.

China: A Society with Common Wealth

First, "common wealth" does not necessarily mean equal wealth, which is hard to achieve in reality. There are significant differences in the development conditions in different regions and there are also differences in human capital among different groups of people. We must objectively recognize such differences and that they are impossible to eliminate. So long as a society exists, there will be social differences.

Second, the core of "common wealth" lies in the word "common," enabling China's vast population to share development opportunities and to improve their development capacity, to raise their development levels, and to share the fruit of development. Only by sharing these aspects in common is it possible to have "common wealth" in its real sense.

Third, "common wealth" decries polarization. We need not worry about the speed of the economic growth, because China is in its take-off stage. What is most concerning is whether China will be able to maintain long-term stability and long-term harmony. The purpose of holding aloft the banner of "common wealth" is to prevent social upheaval and social revolution. "Common wealth" not only serves the political legality of the Communist Party of China in governing the country for the people and invigorating the nation, but is also a political guarantee for long-term peace and social stability. We are not only materialists, objectively recognizing social disparities, but also dialectical materialists, encouraging the people to create wealth quickly *and* encouraging all people to follow the road to common wealth.

Common Prosperity for China and the World

China and the rest of the world are both a community of shared interest and a community of destiny. The opening of China and the increasingly integrated world cannot be separated. Only when the world has become fully developed will it be possible for China to achieve greater development; once the world has become equally prosperous, it will be possible for China to obtain higher levels of prosperity; only when the world obtains greater wealth, especially the developing countries, will it be possible for China to be wealthier. We believe this to be China's relationship with the wider development of the rest of the world.

It is, therefore, necessary to unify both international and domestic situations, and to actively address and manage international challenges. It is possible to turn challenges into opportunities and to create conditions suitable for development by using the advantages offered by both international and domestic resources, and by making better use of international and domestic markets, resources, and technologies. Not only should we offer "invitations" but also take chances and "step outside." Not only should we look after our own affairs but we should also undertake greater international responsibilities. Not only should we participate in globalization, but we should also be global leaders. We should take into consideration both our own development needs and the justifiable concerns of cooperative partners to expand common interests and create win-win situations. We should strive to promote political equality and mutual trust, and promote mutual economic benefits and win-win situations among all countries. We should strive to promote cultural exchange and mutual borrowing combined with dialogue and coordination amongst countries. We should promote the idea that all countries should share in development opportunities, make common efforts to take up challenges, and strive to build a harmonious world, a green world living in lasting peace and common prosperity.

Co-existence and Prosperity Between Man and Nature

China's core national interests, as well as the basic national policies for long-term development, include the saving of resources, environmental protection, ecological security, and the mitigation and prevention of disasters. We must transition from 'black' industrialization, urbanization, and modernization toward green industrialization, urbanization and modernization; from 'black' manufacturing to green manufacturing, from 'black' energy to green energy; from 'black' trade to green trade; from 'black' cities to green cities; and from 'black' consumption to green consumption. This transition can be sustained by ensuring the following five pillars: a resource-efficient society, an environment-friendly society, a cyclic economy, a climate-adaptive society, and an integrated disaster prevention and mitigation strategy.

By tackling global climate change, developing a green economy and green industries, investing in green energy sources, and promoting green consumption, we can greatly improve the quality of economic growth, promote social welfare, and realize economic development, environmental protection, ecological security, and climate adaptation. At the same time, as the most populous country with the largest economic aggregate and creation patents, China is certain to make major contributions to the world's efforts to tackle climate change via peaceful development and green development, and by engaging in international cooperation and green cooperation.

"Common wealth"—China's dream fully embodies traditional ideals of the Chinese people and socialist elements, but the dream is also endowed with new concepts from modern times. To firmly and unswervingly follow the socialist road with unique Chinese characteristics is to follow the road toward common prosperity, firmly and unswervingly.

China's Roadmap

Our definition of "China Road" comes from the book *China 2020: Building a Complete Well-off Society* (Angang Hu 2007). It is defined as a "path to socialist modernization with Chinese characteristics" and contains three basic elements.

The first element is to continuously increase China's modernization factors, expanding production to its maximum to create wealth. China must use up-to-the-minute information, science and technology, and education factors to its best advantage. In essence, China, as a late-comer and a laggard in the quest for modernization, will be locked in a process of constant catching up with developed countries in terms of economy, education, science and technology, and information and communications technologies.

The second element is to continuously increase socialist elements, seeking common development, common sharing, and common prosperity by showcasing the superiority of China's socialist and political system. This is the legacy left by Mao Zedong. Only by constantly increasing socialist elements will it be possible to rally China's population of more than one billion people, and to mobilize all possible facets of society. Only by adhering to the basic political system of socialism, will it be possible to realize political national unity and a strong unified plural country able to enjoy long-term peace and security.

The third element is to continuously increase Chinese culture, providing major innovations in pursuing an ideal society containing strong Chinese characteristics. Thus, China will create a prosperous society, a harmonious society, a learning society, and a society in which people will live and work in peace and happiness. We can sum up the concept of a modern socialist society with Chinese characteristics as "eight societies and one road." The purpose is to enable all people to execute their roles, "turning human resources to their best account." Another important principle is to exert unprecedented influence on the world as a whole in terms of peace, development, and cooperation.

These three elements determine China's roadmap for development and the upgrading and regeneration of the Chinese vision.

The modernization element shows that China's development roadmap needs to develop China first from an underdeveloped country to a mid-level developed country. Then, China can transition to a relatively developed country, and ultimately to a highly developed country, a country with high income, high human development, and high welfare.

As far as the socialist element is concerned, China will develop from an immature socialist state, to a relatively mature system, and then to a more advanced level of socialism. In the 1950s, China spent a relatively short time establishing its basic system of socialism, which is neither mature nor developed. This led to the catastrophe of the "Great Leap Forward" and the internal upheaval of the "Great Cultural Revolution." Thus, the superiority of socialism has not been showcased. It was not until the 1980s that it was realized that China was still at a primary stage of socialism, that is, an underdeveloped stage. China has, however, become relatively mature over time and enjoys a degree of successful socialism, but the system is still not perfect. While the socialist system in China is still at a primary stage, it will advance in the future to a mature and then a fully developed stage.

When viewed from the perspective of Chinese culture, China's road has its sources, heredity, progressiveness, rationale, and its sense of justice from history. China has developed from a poverty-stricken nation to a stage where there was enough food and clothing for all, and is now a prosperous society, and next its society will enter into a period of great harmony. First, China shook off poverty, resolving the problem of inadequate food and clothing for its population of more than one billion people, and then went on to raise its citizens' living standards and to improve the material and cultural conditions of all. China will ultimately realize its dream society of great harmony with common wealth, equality, and benefit for all.

The evolution of the New China shows that China's road is a road to socialist modernization with Chinese characteristics. This was described in a report to the 17th National Party Congress, which stated that all the achievements and progress since the reform and opening up were as a result of China blazing a path to socialism with specific Chinese characteristics and, theoretically, establishing a system of socialist theories with Chinese characteristics. This is China's most significant innovation to date, both in practice and in theory. This is a path to common wealth and a world of great harmony. To date, China has provided its citizens with a comfortable standard of living and is currently building its prosperous society. It is certain to realize the ideal of common prosperity.

The trajectory of China's socialist modernization is not straight or pre-designed. It is a course marked with constant exploration, summing-up, opening-up, and changes. The years since the founding of the country show that China has experienced three generations of development approaches: the Mao Zedong era, the Deng Xiaoping and Jiang Zemin era, and the Hu Jintao and post-Hu era. The different eras are simply the upgrading of China's "software" regarding socialist modernization as there are always uncertainties, incompleteness, certain incompatibilities, and disharmony with information and knowledge in reality when the "software" is designed and developed. It has to be improved, added to, and refurbished, hence the inter-connected upgrade of the versions. In other words, the former edition is the basis of the later editions, and the later editions are the repairs, modifications, and upgrading of the previous versions—the socialist modernization with Chinese characteristics Version 1.0, Version 2.0, and Version 3.0.

The essence of China's road is a roadmap of modernization with Chinese characteristics. It encompasses four steps in terms of development level and stages. The first step (1978–1990) covered the transition from absolute poverty to a level of adequate food and clothing; the second step (1990–2000) covered the transition from adequate food and clothing to prosperous living conditions; the third step (2000–2020) covers the transition from prosperous living conditions to a prosperous society; and the fourth step (2020–2030)will cover the transition from a prosperous society to a society of common wealth. The achievement of these four steps will complete the modernization of the populous country, which accounts for one-fifth of the world's total population. In terms of national power, China first became a world power (ranking among the top 10 in 1978), and then moved to the front ranks (among the top five in 2000), and advanced to the No. 2 position (2010). China will become the world No. 1 (by 2020) and will be the most powerful country in the world. In terms of life cycle, it is estimated that China's dominance will last more than 100 years. However, this will, of course, depend on the following generations, who will be wiser than those of the present day. The author of this roadmap is Mao Zedong and the earliest architect is Deng Xiaoping. China has been following this route for some time, changing from the "sick man of East Asia" to the "giant of the East." This is, in itself, the original road of China.

China's road has never been straight, but filled with twists and turns. It is a road like the Long March, filled with hardships and challenges. China is rapidly developing and changing, and growing more open. It is a typical dual society: it has both a bright and dark side, with the bright side overshadowing the dark; it has both a positive and negative side, with the positive always overwhelming the negative; and it has a progressive side and a decadent side, with the progressive side overpowering the decadent side. History has proved, as will the future, that China's road is an inevitable road in realizing socialist modernization, an inevitable road in creating a beautiful life for the people, and an inevitable road in the great rejuvenation of the Chinese nation (Hu Jintao 2011).

Logic of China's Development

From the mid-1990s to the mid-twentieth century, China remained a laggard in the drive for worldwide modernization and was subject to bullying. In the latter half of the twentieth century, China played a successful game of catch up, advancing from behind to stand at the international front. Entering the twenty-first century, China will catch up with and overtake the most developed capitalist country in the world, the United States.[11] This will occur not only because of China's 1 billion population, 9.6 million square meters of territorial land, and several thousand years of civilization, culture, and written language, but also because China has its uniquely superior socialist system, which includes both the superiority of the fundamental political system of socialism and the advantages of the socialist economic market system.

How will we predict China's prospects regarding future development? The prediction records on China's development both at home and abroad over the past decades show that neo-classical growth theory is, in reality, unable to predict the development of China's economy. Predictions by many economic models, no matter how precise or complicated they are, have been proven far from accurate, with most models significantly underestimating the potential of China's development.

---

[11] In December 1962, Zhou Enlai pointed out "It is a matter of course for the late comer to catch up. Our country has many advantages and we should be more confident of catching up with and overtake the scientifically and technically advanced countries in not a too long time. (Mao Zedong's words) Simply put, we must spend dozens of years catching up with and surpassing the level that took western bourgeoisie several hundred years to attain" (Zhou Enlai 1964).

In contrast, Mao Zedong, Deng Xiaoping, and other Chinese leaders have offered accurate presages and predictions regarding the prospects of China's development. These leaders did not rely on specialized knowledge and tools, but rather on their political wisdom and wealth of experience.

We have looked to the experience of Mao Zedong and Deng Xiaoping in our predictions and concepts for 2030. We have pinpointed the crucial variables that will influence China's long-term development and carried out an in-depth analysis of the major problems and contradictions. Thus, we have conceived China's future in a bold and forward-looking manner, based on both economic analysis and long-term development experience, with a focus on the orientation of China's future development strategy. Although we are faced with many uncertainties regarding the future, we are most concerned about the following questions: What is the most significant opportunity for the future? Which prediction is the most accurate and how can it be put into practice and tested in the future?

China is conscientious and not reckless in its development; the development is purposeful and not spontaneous, planned and not disorderly. The development represents the integration of three trends: a natural (objective) trend, market-driven development under the guidance of plans, and development under the guidance of planning and strategy. To predict China's development, it is necessary to take into account the interactions among the three trends.

The value of an objective trend is the result of spontaneous behavior subject to society. This reflects the interaction between the indicators and the development stage; that is, the trend changes with an increase in per capita income or per capita GDP, and has nothing to do with the variables of government policies. With regard to the value of an objective trend, it is necessary to consider the various influencing factors, including the basic national conditions, development stage and development potential, and all uncertainties and restraining factors. Only then can forward-looking predictions and scientific calculations be made.

A market driven value is subject to guidance by government policies in the process of planning to excite market initiatives and, therefore, mobilize the forces of society as a whole to accelerate the realization of the state objectives. However, in many circumstances, non-governmental and market forces would far exceed the anticipation and expectations of government. Of course, the objectives (to some degree) are also subject to the impact of external resistance in the process of development, and are discounted to an extent. Thus, the market driven value is reduced, even to zero in some cases. Nevertheless, due to the constraint of the third factor, plan guidance value, these objectives will ultimately have their bottom line.

The plan guidance value is the government influence on the real development trend indicators by reasonably allocating public resources and effectively employing public forces to either accelerate development (developmental indicator) or to limit the development trend (control type indicator). It reflects the role of the visible hand of government planning. Plan guidance value determines the intensity of the political will on the one hand and on the other it is based on the drawing capacity of public resources (financial, material, and human resources), the capacity of mobilization, and the allocation capacity.

The above three trends also reflect China's superiority regarding both development and system. In terms of developmental superiority, China has an advantage as a latecomer, large-scale power efficiency, and significant development potential, accompanied by fairly long periods of development opportunities. China has the momentum and conditions for high-speed development. In terms of system, China has the advantage of the "invisible hand" of the market drive, which is full of vitality and creativity, and the advantage of the "visible hand" in terms of long-term development strategy and planning. The organic combination of the two, in turn, will accelerate the development speed and at the same time competently direct development.

This book focuses on the three major trends outlined above to predict the development trends for both China and the world. First, we make a prediction regarding the natural growth trends for all indicators using a linear model. Second, an adjustment is made for the estimated linear values for 2015 or 2020, based on already published development plans, and judgments are then made regarding the long-term trend for 2030 using a rule of thumb. An estimation of population growth and population structure is a core clue to predict the long-term development of both China and the world, and is the basis for accurate predictions.

Theme and Structure of the Book

This book seeks to answer the following questions: What is the China of 2030? What changes will occur with regard to the disparities between man and man, between man and nature, and between China and the world? What is "common prosperity and a world of great harmony"? Can China's 2030 blueprint become a reality, and if so, how?

This book presents a clear blueprint for China up to the year 2030: a China that has been resolutely, boldly, and meticulously designed. This book will describe to the world a China of the future. It is a development program and it openly expresses the ideas, development objectives, and development strategies for China 2030.

Chapter 2 provides an introduction, which clearly states China's dream of "common prosperity and a world of great harmony." China has the will, the conditions, and capabilities to make this dream come true because of the superiority of its socialist system and development, and because of its enviable state of "good opportunities, and favorable geographical and human conditions."

Chapter 3 presents a world view for 2030. It highlights our visions for the world and our predictions for worldwide future developments. Our predictions are optimistic, because southern countries are rising and the world is moving toward a golden age of development. Furthermore, the world is currently enjoying an unprecedented era of common prosperity. Our aim is globalism, pursuing "world peace," with the aim of breaking down the existing imbalanced and unjust international order to realize common development and common prosperity.

Chapter 4 predicts that China will become a modern economic power by 2030. It holds that China will continue to maintain a 7–8% growth rate over the next 20 years and China's main reliance will shift from factor inputs to mainly total factor productivity. China will become the largest consumer market, with the largest modern industrial system, the largest urbanization area, with the largest and most modern infrastructure system in the world.

Chapter 5 predicts that China will become an innovative global power by 2030 in areas of human resources, science and technology, and information and communications technology. China will enter an era that will see its population of more than one billion become involved in innovative development, and they will become the driving force behind China's development. Essentially, China will become a leading competitive power.

Chapter 6 predicts that China will become a country characterized by high levels of welfare by 2030, enjoying high income, high levels of education, and high life expectancy. It will become a country with high levels of human development and China's people will enjoy high levels of happiness.

Chapter 7 predicts that China will become a country with common prosperity by 2030. This includes reducing the three major disparities, that is, disparity between town and country, disparity among regions, and income disparity. In addition, public services will become more equal and everyone will be able to enjoy basic social security.

Chapter 8 describes China as a green China in 2030, with comprehensive ecological profits. It will become the world's largest green energy system, free from carbon emissions. It will become an environment-friendly society with low disaster risks. It will become a beautiful homeland for China's people.

Thus, by 2030 China's dream of common prosperity and a world of great harmony will come true. China will represent a new type of superpower, not only economically but also in terms of innovation. At the same time, China will be a relatively developed country by 2030, with per capita income, education levels, health levels, and a human development index close to those of developed countries. China will remain a country with harmonious relations between man and nature, a country sharing common prosperity, and a country that will make greater innovative contributions, green contributions, and contributions to the civilization of humanity.

This book is an integrated innovative work on the future development prospects of China and the world as a whole. The information contained within has been sourced from two central resources. The first is from the main reports and plans of the Communist Party of China and the Chinese government. These include the following: the report to the 16th National Party Congress (2002), the report to the 17th National Party Congress (2007), the outline program of the 11th five-year plan for economic and social development (2006), the outline program of the 12th five-year plan for economic and social development (2011), the country's long- and medium-term development programs in particular areas, such as the outline program for the medium- and long-term development of science and technology for 2006–2020 (2006), outline program for medium- and long-term personnel development 2011–2020 (2010), and the outline program for the planning of main functional zones 2011–2020 (2011).

The second source of information comes from the achievements of both domestic and foreign research institutions. These include the following research and institutions:

"Innovation 2050: Science and Technology Revolution and China's Future" by the China's Academy of Sciences (2009); Li Shantong's "China's Economy by 2030" (2010); World Bank's "China 2020"; Roland Berger's "Trends 2007–2030"; Chartered Bank's "The Super-Cycle Report"; "Global Trends 2025: A Transformed World" by the National Intelligence Council of the United States: FBI's "World Fact Book 2011"; and International Energy Agency's "World Energy Outlook 2011." We have also made full use of the UN population databank, the databank of the UN Trade and Development Council, the databank of the World Bank on world development indicators, the databank of the World Trade Organization and the databank of Augus Maddison's history of the World Economy.

References

Angang Hu (2002) Construct China's Grand Strategy: Grandiose objective of making people prosper and the country strong. China Studies special, Nov 2002

Angang Hu (2007) China 2020: building a complete well-off society. Tsinghua University Press, Beijing

Deng Xiaoping (1993a) We should take a longer-range view in developing Sino-Japanese relations, March 25, 1984. In: Selected works of Deng Xiaoping, vol 3. People's Publishing House, Beijing, p 54

Deng Xiaoping (1993b) Seize the opportunity to develop the economy, December 24, 1990. In: Selected works of Deng Xiaoping, vol 3. People's Publishing House, Beijing, p 364, edition

Deng Xiaoping (1993c) Take a clear-cut stand against bourgeois liberalization, December 30, 1986. In: Selected works of Deng Xiaoping, vol 3. People's Publishing House, Beijing, p 195

Deng Xiaoping (1993d) Draw on historical experience and prevent erroneous tendencies, April 30, 1987. In: Selected works of Deng Xiaoping, vol 3. People's Publishing House, Beijing, p 226

Deng Xiaoping (1994a) China's goal is to achieve comparative prosperity by the end of the century, Dec. 6, 1979. In: Selected works of Deng Xiaoping, vol 2. People's Publishing House, Beijing, p 237

Deng Xiaoping (1994b) Complement the policy of readjustment and ensure stability and unity, Dec. 25, 1980. In: Selected works of Deng Xiaoping, vol 2. People's Publishing House, Beijing, p 356

Hu Jintao (2007) Hold high the great banner of socialism with Chinese characteristics and strive for new victories in building a moderately prosperous society in all respects, Oct 15, 2007. Xinhua News Agency, Beijing, Oct 24

Hu Jintao (2011) Speech at the mass rally marking the 90th anniversary of the founding of the Communist Party of China, 1 July 2011

Jiang Zemin (2002) Building a well-off society in all aspects and opening new ground in the socialist cause with Chinese Characteristics – Report to the 16th National Congress of the Communist Party of China, October 15, 2002, carried in CPC Central Research Office: Selected Important Documents Since the 16th National Party Congress (Part I). Central Documentation Press, Beijing, 2005, pp 14–16

Kang Youwei (1994) The book of great harmony. Liaoning People's Publishing House, Shenyang

Lin Zhaomu (2007) Looking to China after it realizes the 2020 Goal. Reading guide to 17th national party congress report. People's Publishing House, Beijing, pp 92–93

Liu He (2007) Get a correct command of the new requirements for building a well-off society. Reading guide to 17th national party congress report. People's Publishing House, Beijing, p 87

Mao Zedong (1991) On people's democratic dictatorship. In: Selected works of Mao Zedong, vol 4. People's Publishing House, Beijing, p 1471

Mao Zedong (1999a) Speech at the enlarged central work conference (January 30, 1962). In: Collected works of Mao Zedong, vol 8. People's Publishing House, Beijing, p 302

Mao Zedong (1999b) Speech at a forum on the socialist transformation of capitalist industry and commerce, Oct. 29, 1955. In: Collected works of Mao Zedong, vol 6. People's Publishing House, Beijing, pp 495–496

Sun Wen (1924) Three principles of the people. Hanwen Library

World Bank Economic Study Tour (1983) China: socialist economic development, Chinese edn. China Finance and Economic Press, Beijing

Zeng Peiyan (2009) Main tasks of economic development and reform for the first two decades of the new century. Reading guide to 16th national party congress report. People's Publishing House, Beijing, p 79

Zhou Enlai (1964) Government Work Report, December 21–22, 1964, CPC Central Documentation Office: Selected Important Documents since the founding of New China, vol 19, pp 493–494. Central Documentation Press, Beijing, 1998; CPC Central Documentation Office: Manuscripts of Mao Zedong since the Founding of New China, vol 11. Central Documentation Press, Beijing, 1996, p 272

Chapter 3
A World of Common Prosperity

Peace would then reign over the world,
with all people under heaven to share
the same warmth and cold.

Mao Zedong (1935)

We should look at development issues
in terms of the development of mankind as a whole.
We must observe and resolve problems this way.

Deng Xiaoping (1988); Deng Xiaoping (1993a)

Since the reform and opening up of China more than 30 years ago, the country has been actively involved in the world economy. China has become the biggest beneficiary of economic globalization and has rapidly grown to become the second largest trader (climbing from its original position of 29th place). China will soon overtake the United States to become the world's No. 1 importer and exporter and the bellwether of economic integration and trade liberalization, playing a significant role in the global economic system.

The wider world has influenced China and China has influenced the world; the wider world has changed China and China has changed the world. However, how can we predict long-term worldwide development trends? How should we view the external environment to determine China's future development? How do we understand the interactive relations between China and the rest of the world? What do global development trends mean to China? What challenges does global development bring? What opportunities does global development bring? This chapter will offer some simple conclusions and provide clearer answers to the above questions.

Obtaining a clearer picture of the world situation is an important element in obtaining a deeper understanding and an accurate view of national conditions. We believe that the global economy will enter a new golden growth period between 2010 and 2030. The global industrial structure will continue to adjust and improve; international trade will be liberalized and more integrated; the global investment pattern will become evenly distributed between the South and the North; the world will herald in a new science and technology revolution; the global population will begin to age and urbanization will accelerate; and the global demand for energy and its consumption will undergo an extensive reform in its transition to green energy.

The presence of these factors will mean that the world will undergo a series of major, profound and complicated changes. Peace, development and cooperation will become mainstream and there will be further development for both multi-polarization and economic globalization. The world economic and political patterns will undergo transformations. There will be new breakthroughs in science and technology. The trend of reform will become more and more appropriate for China. When viewing the world as a whole, there will be both opportunities and challenges, with the opportunities overwhelming the challenges and favorable factors overpowering unfavorable factors. The convergence of these elements will create 70 years (1980–2050) of a peaceful international environment as visualized by Deng Xiaoping (see Box 3.1). Thus, China's important strategic period of opportunity in the twenty-first century will not last just 20 years,[1] but rather 30 or even 50 years.

Box 3.1 Deng Xiaoping: "70 Years" of a Peaceful International Environment

China's development strategy from the mid- to late 1970s was, in essence, based on Deng Xiaoping's theory of establishing new international political and economic environments. In 1974, after returning from the United Nations General Assembly in New York, Deng Xiaoping reported to Mao Zedong his new idea for a "five-year international peace" period; that is, China needs 5 years of international peace to further its development. In 1977, Deng Xiaoping announced his quest for "23 years of international peace;" that is, China needs 23 years of a peaceful international environment to aid its development. Then in 1987, Deng Xiaoping further extended the concept to "70 years of international peace;" that is, China will need a long-term peaceful international environment from 1980 to 2050 to realize its "three-step" strategy.

This is Deng Xiaoping's "grand strategy" of China, which fully reflects China's core national interests and long-term fundamental interests in managing relations with other countries. It is a bold and advanced strategic concept. As long as there are 70 years of international peace, China is sure to become the most powerful socialist modernized country in the world and will make major contributions to both world development and to changing the world order of the South and the North.

---

[1] The report to the 16th National Party Congress points out that in the first 20 years of the twenty-first century, we must come to grips with the important strategic period of opportunity in which we will have plenty of room to display our talents (Jiang Zemin 2002).

A Golden Period for the Global Economy

Since the nineteenth century, the world has experienced two golden ages of economic growth (by a golden age of growth, we mean an uninterrupted and stable growth cycle in the global economy, usually lasting for more than 10 years).[2] The first was from 1870 to 1913, marked by the electrical and rail revolutions, when the United States and Western European countries were dominant.[3] The second was from 1950 to 1973.[4]

The period from 1990 to 2030 will see the world in its third golden age of economic growth. From 1990 to 2030, the world economy is expected to maintain an annual growth of approximately 3.0–3.5%.[5] Many countries will be included in the new golden age, as well as millions of people. The current levels of economic globalization and integration are so high that they cannot be compared to the previous two golden ages.[6] The third golden age will include more than 200 countries

---

[2] The British Standard Chartered Bank put forward the concept of "super cycle," which is similar to the golden growth period. It defines a cycle as "a period of historically high global growth, lasting a generation or more, driven by increasing trade, high rates of investment, urbanization and technological innovation, characterized by the emergence of large, new economies, first seen in high catch-up growth rates across the emerging world." See the Standard Chartered Bank, the "Super Cycle Report," 2010.

[3] Angus Maddison holds that this is a period of relative peace and prosperity, with the world's GDP growing at an average annual rate of 2.1%, higher than the 1820–1870 growth (1.0%). In addition, per capita GDP growth at 1.3%, is also higher than the 1820–1870 rate (0.6%) (see Maddison 1995).

[4] Angus Maddison holds that this is the golden period with unprecedented prosperity, with the world GDP growing at an average annual rate of 4.9% and per capita GDP at 2.9%. These rates are higher than in any previous historical period. World exports grew by 7.0%. The United States and Europe have played positive roles in the diffusion of technology, benefiting Western Europe, southern Europe, and Asia (see Maddison 1995).

[5] Scholars and research institutions have basically gone along with the view that the global economy will maintain its rapid growth over the next 20 years. The Standard Chartered Bank report points out that 2000–2030 will be the third super cycle since the industrial revolution in the West. The global economy will maintain 2.7% growth per annum. The previous super cycles were in 1870–1913 and 1946–1973, in which the global economy grew at an average annual rate of 2.7% and 5.0%, respectively. See the Standard Chartered Bank, "The Super Cycle Report 2010". Roland Berger states in its report that from 2007 to 2030, the global economy will maintain approximately 3% growth, with the economic aggregate doubling in approximately 23 years. See Roland Berger, "Trend 2030," 2007. Even the National Intelligence Council of the United States holds that in 2010–2025, global economic growth may reach 4% (see National Intelligence Council 2008). Economic historian Maddison also holds that the most successful three periods of economic development were 1870–1913, a free order period, 1950–1973, a golden age, and 1973 and onward, which is a new liberal order. In his works, he estimates that in 2003–2030, world GDP will be 2.2%, with wealthy countries at 0.7%, and other countries, 3.3% (see Maddison 2003, 2008).

[6] More than 20 countries were involved in the first golden age, including those in Western Europe and the United States, with a total population of 400 million in 1870, accounting for 31.9% of the global population. More than 40 countries and regions were involved in the second golden age, including those in North America and Europe (excluding Eastern Europe), Japan, Israel, the Republic of Korea, and Hong Kong, with a total population of 980 million in 1973, representing 25% of the world's population.

Table 3.1 Global economic growth cycle (1820–2030)

Period	Average growth (%)	Growth fluctuation coefficient
1820–1870	0.9	0.29
1870–1913	2.1	0.42
1913–1950	0.2	13.81
1950–1973	4.9	0.21
1973–1990	3.0	0.42
1990–2030	3.5	–

Note: The annual average growth coefficient for 2011–2030 is an estimate of the author
Sources: Angus Maddison, Statistics on World Population, GDP and Per Capita GDP, 1–2008 AD,
2010, http://www.ggdc.net/MADDISON/oriindex.htm

Table 3.2 Global economic growth and sources (1990–2030)

Unit: %

	1990–2010	2010–2030	1990–2030
GDP	3.1	3.5	3.3
Capital input	2.5	3.5	3.0
Labor input	1.7	0.1	0.9
Human capital input	1.2	1.2	1.2
TFP	1.2	1.7	1.5

Note: The weight of capital input is 0.4, labor input 0.3, and human capital input 0.3. Total factor
productivity (TFP). The data in the table are the estimates of the author
Sources: Figures for 1990–2010 GDP growth, capital input growth (average growth of fixed assets
formed) and labor increases are calculated based on data from the World Development Indicator
2011. Figures for human capital input growth are calculated based on Robert J. Barro and Jong-
Wha Lee, A New Data Set of Educational Attainment in the World, 1950–2010, NBER Working
Paper No. 15902, 2010

and regions, and a total population of approximately 6–7 billion people. The third
golden age will be characterized as involving an extensive period of high-speed
growth, and on a massive scale (see Table 3.1).

In terms of economic growth sources, the important factors to sustain the global
golden age will be TFP growth fueled by science, technology, and innovation, and
the growth of human capital reserves fueled by education (see Table 3.2).

We estimate that from 2000 to 2030, approximately half of the global economic
growth will come from an increase in TFP, as it benefits from industrial restructuring, technical progress, and the integration of the world economy.

Human capital investment will be the powerful kingpin of rapid global economic
growth for some time to come.[7] The global investment in human capital is shifting
from elementary education, to mid-level education, on to higher education. The number

---

[7] The average years of education in developed countries has increased from 6.22 in 1950 to 7.76 in
2010, an average annual growth of 1.0%. The average years of education for developing countries
has increased from 2.05 in 1950 to 7.09 in 2010, an average annual growth of 2.1% (Barro and
Jong-Wha 2010).

of people receiving higher education will grow rapidly. In China alone, the number of people with at least a high school education will increase from 120 million in 2010 to more than 300 million by 2030. Not only will the number of laborers with higher levels of education increase by a substantial margin, but also labor productivity.[8]

The development levels of emerging economies will also rise, with an obvious effect on capital brought about by the transition of the domestic industry. Thus, there will be a steady growth in material capital inputs.

India, and other up-and-coming countries, will still be able to provide enough labor during this stage. The global working age population for 2010–2030 will sit at approximately 65%, higher than the rates of 60.5 and 57.6% in 1950 and 1975, respectively, and will be at its highest level since 1950.

In the current golden age of economic development, there will be major changes in the global economic landscape. The economic strength of the South and the North will be reversed. Not only will China and India return to 1820 levels by 2030, all countries of the South will return to 1820 levels, representing a typical U-turn.

The rapid rise of the South has meant that as of 2010 the South is now bigger (52.4%) than the North (47.6%); this is an obvious change in the status quo where the North had dominated the world economic order. By 2030, the South could represent 66.9% of countries and the North could be further reduced to 33.1%. The South could dominate the world economy.

The countries of the South will enjoy the full dividends of world peace, as well as the dividends of economic globalization and integration. The spread and sharing of development knowledge will enable developing countries to increase their governance abilities. In addition, innovation, diffusion, and sharing, and improvements to communication infrastructures, especially information infrastructures, will stimulate the collective rise of the South. We are now at the mid-point of this period of growth. This trend is now commonplace worldwide, albeit accompanied by tributaries; this is a worldwide trend with local counter-currents. Although this is an irreversible worldwide trend, there may still be international financial crises. We are seeing more and more countries becoming involved in this mainstream trend.

Emerging economies have become a fresh motivating force behind global economic growth. China, in particular, is both the biggest beneficiary and the greatest supporter of the golden age of world economic development. From 2000 to 2030, countries with massive populations, such as Brazil, Russia, India, and China (BRIC), will become the central forces propelling global economic growth. By 2030, it is possible that the BRIC countries will have a combined economic aggregate representing 60.1% of the world's total. That of China's alone will exceed the combined total of the North (see Table 3.3).

In contrast, the economic aggregates of the United States, the EU, and Japan will drop from 18.4, 18.1, and 5.4%, to 15.1, 13.1, and 3.2%, respectively. By 2030, the

---

[8] Robert Fogel points out in his research that the productivity of a laborer with at least a college education, is three times that of a laborer with an elementary and middle school education (Fogel 2008).

Table 3.3 World total GDP (PPP) percentages for the South and the North (1820–2030)

Unit: %

	1820	1870	1913	1950	1973	2000	2010	2020	2030
The South	**70.3**	**53.1**	**42.1**	**39.5**	**39.9**	**43.0**	**52.4**	**60.5**	**66.9**
Developing Asian countries	56.5	36.1	22.2	15.3	15.8	29.2	40.9	49.1	58.2
China	33.0	17.1	8.8	4.6	4.6	11.8	20.7	28.9	33.4
India	16.1	12.2	7.5	4.2	3.1	5.2	8.0	12.2	18.6
Russia	5.4	7.5	8.5	9.6	9.4	2.1	2.4	2.7	3.0
Brazil	0.4	0.6	0.7	1.7	2.5	2.7	2.6	3.6	5.1
The North	**29.7**	**46.9**	**57.9**	**60.5**	**60.1**	**57.0**	**47.6**	**39.5**	**33.1**
USA	1.8	8.9	18.9	27.3	22.1	21.9	18.4	16.7	15.1
EU	23.3	32.0	35.8	27.1	27.1	21.5	18.1	15.7	13.1
Japan	3.0	2.3	2.6	3.0	7.8	7.2	5.4	4.4	3.2
China/USA	**18.3**	**1.9**	**0.47**	**0.17**	**0.2**	**0.5**	**1.1**	**1.7**	**2.2**

Note: The North refers to advanced economies as defined by the IMF. They include 34 countries; the EU includes 27 countries that are not included in the North; developing Asian countries refers to Asian countries other than Japan, South Korea, Singapore, Chinese Hong Kong, and Israel; GDP (PPP) is in 1990 international dollars

Sources: Data for 1820–2000 was sourced from Angus Maddison, Statistics on World Population, GDP and Per Capita GDP, 1–2008 AD, 2010, for http://www.ggdc.net/MADDISON/orindex.htm Data regarding growth from 2010 to 2030 for the world and major economies are the estimates of the author

Table 3.4 Global industrial structure (1960-2030)

Unit: %						
	1960	1980	2000	2010	2020	2030
Agriculture	8.8	6.6	3.6	2.9	2.4	2.1
Industry	38.2	37.0	28.9	27.0	22.1	20.0
Manufacturing	29.0	25.1	19.2	16.8	12.4	11.2
Service	53.0	56.4	67.5	70.2	75.6	77.9

Note: Data for 2020–2030 are the estimates of the author
Source: World Bank, World Development Indicators 2011

five biggest world economies will be those of China, India, the United States, the EU, and Brazil.[9]

The global golden age is an important development opportunity for the world; for China, it is an important period of strategic opportunity. It will provide China with a rare international environment, ripe for development. It is a window for China to make full use of international peace and resources to realize its own development. It will enable the expansion of China's development opportunities, and give China the room to expand into the world market and into the international arena.

Period of Global Industrial Restructuring

The structure of global industry will change, with a reduction in the proportion of agriculture and industry (especially manufacturing), but accompanied by a significant increase in the service industry.[10] This adjustment and subsequent upgrading of the structures within developing countries will see more and more labor transferred into industry and service fields. These areas will become the main employment structure, and that in agriculture will be significantly reduced (see Table 3.4).

The main reason for the reduction in the percentage of industry, especially manufacturing, and the sustained rise in services is the result of a steady increase in manufacturing capital, which increases labor productivity in the service sector. In addition, the increase in the tradability of manufactured goods in the international trade system will ultimately be concentrated in those countries with the strongest

---

[9] This prediction is similar to the 2007 prediction by Nobel laureate Robert Fogel, who said that by 2040 the economic aggregates of the United States, the EU (15 countries), India, China, and Japan will be 14%, 5%, 12%, 40%, and 2%, respectively (see Fogel 2007).

[10] Regarding the structure of global industry, industry peaked in 1970, accounting for 38.7% of the industry structure, before falling steadily (especially after 1980). The manufacturing peak occurred in the 1960s, accounting for 29.0% of industry. By 2030, the percentage of agriculture will be at 2.1% and industry at 20%, of which manufacturing will account for 11.2% while service will make up 77.9%. According to the US CIA World Factbook, in 2006 the percentages of those employed in agriculture, industry, and service were 36.6, 21.5, and 41.9%, respectively.

comparative advantages. Tourism, communications and transport, information and telecommunications, and financial and insurance services will be the biggest contributors. These services will become the central forces behind the development of international service trade. The proportion of knowledge services will rapidly increase to become a motivating force in both long-term national growth and the transition toward a knowledge-based economy and society.

In the process of restructuring, mature developed economies will basically retain their existing industrial structure and their domination of services will be further strengthened. The industrial structures of emerging countries will undergo drastic changes, with the percentage of agricultural industry and employment reducing further. Any surviving agricultural production will be modernized. The percentage of industries that are capital-intensive, energy and water sapping, heavy consumers of resources, and heavily polluting will significantly reduce. In contrast, labor- and knowledge-intensive services and those in the area of energy conservation and emissions reduction will enjoy significant increases. Labor-intensive industries will be largely transferred to Africa (south of the Sahara), where the percentage of industry will rise.

A drop in the percentage of agriculture means that the dependency on scarce agricultural resources will also reduce. A reduction in the percentage of industry will produce a significant reduction in the dependency on non-renewable energy sources and raw materials. A rapid rise in the percentage of services will represent an increase in the dependency of the economic system on various knowledge factors, including, science and technology, education, and information. These factors will become the driving forces behind economic growth and employment. Knowledge will be characterized by a progressive increase of marginal returns, which differs from both agricultural and industrial production factors. Knowledge can be easily spread and disseminated, which is significant in tackling global climate change.[11]

Intensification of International Economic Integration

International economic integration manifests itself in the integration of international trade and in the integration of international investment. The global trade volume will continue to maintain its high-speed growth and the integration of international and domestic markets will continue to rise. The momentum of the high-speed growth experienced in international trade since World War II will be maintained. From 1950 to 2010, the average worldwide annual growth in exports was 6.8%, reaching approximately US$16 trillion in 2010, 31.2% of global GDP. By 2030, global exports are expected to break the US$55 trillion dollar mark to reach 53.4%

---

[11] For example, regarding services other than communications, their outputs by 2030 will account for more than 50% of the global GDP, but carbon emissions will only account for 2.7% of the global total (see International Energy Agency 2011a).

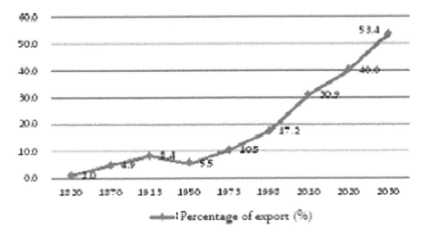

Fig. 3.1 Global Export in Global GDP (%) (Note: Data for 2010 are the estimates of the author. The annual average growth of exports for 2010–2030 is estimated at 6.2%. Exports include goods and services. Data for export and GDP values are in 1990 international dollars; Sources: Maddison 2001; WTO, International Trade Statistics, 2010)

of global GDP. The most conservative estimate is that global exports will grow at an average annual rate of approximately 6.4% during this period (see Fig. 3.1).

Emerging countries will play an increasingly important role in the international trade system, ending the long-term domination of the North. First, the world factory will be transferred from the North to the South. In 1870, the ratio of international exports between the South and the North was essentially 30:70. In 2010, the ratio was 40:60. By 2030 it will be 70:30. By then, China's total exports will be close to a quarter of the world's total (see Table 3.5). Then, the world market will also be transferred from the North to the South. In 1950, the ratio of the South and the North in international imports was 30:70. By 2020 it will be 50:50, and 60:40 by 2030. By then, China's total imports will be more than a quarter of the world's total, becoming a net importer instead of net exporter (see Table 3.6).

In the international trade system, agricultural trade will increase but the percentage will continue to drop and service trades will rapidly increase, with its percentage of total international trade to increase from 20% (currently) to approximately 30%.

Trade liberalization will remain a mainstream worldwide trend; however, this will be accompanied by a long-term conflict between trade liberalization and trade protectionism. Country-specific trade friction cannot be avoided. There is even the possibility of an outbreak of local or regional trade wars, with the world powers being both interdependent and locked in such conflict.

Until 2030, China will have a double role in world trade and investments: China will be transformed from a net exporter to a net importer, and from a net investment inflow country to a net outflow country. China will always be an active supporter and actor in trade liberalization, stimulating trade liberalization, a fair trading system, and mutual benefit trading instead of the concept of trade liberalization pursued in the West. China has enabled and will further enable developing countries to gain from trade liberalization and globalization. The Doha round of negotiations by the World Trade Organization (WTO), have seen the environment and order of international trade improve, and further improvements are expected. For China, its opportunities in the international trade system far outweigh any possible challenges. In the future trading system, importers will be the winners. China will enjoy market advantages. The transition from "a Chinese factory" to "a Chinese market" will further strengthen the position and role of China in the international trade system.

From 2010 to 2030, Global investments will maintain a certain growth rate, most likely at the 3% annual growth that has been registered since the beginning of the 1990s. Newly added foreign investments will mainly come from the emerging markets of China, India, Brazil, and Russia.

Global foreign investment will be characterized by the interaction between the inflow and outflow of foreign direct investment, with a transition of investment from developed countries to developing countries and from developing countries to developed countries.

Table 3.5 Total global export percentages for the South and the North (1870–2030)

Unit: %

	1870	1950	1973	1998	2010	2020	2030
The South	**28.1**	**37.6**	**39.2**	**41.4**	**62.2**	**68.0**	**72.0**
China	2.8	2.1	0.7	3.3	10.4	18.0	24.0
India	6.9	1.9	0.6	0.7	1.4	2.4	5.0
Russia	0.0	2.2	3.4	2.1	2.5	2.7	3.5
Brazil	1.7	1.2	0.6	0.9	1.3	1.7	2.9
The North	**71.9**	**62.4**	**60.8**	**58.6**	**37.8**	**32.0**	**28.0**
USA	5.0	14.6	10.3	12.8	8.4	10.0	9.0
EU	60.4	38.9	43.2	38.1	15.7	14.0	12.0
Japan	0.1	1.2	5.6	5.9	5.1	5.0	4.0

Table 3.6 Total global export percentages for the South and the North (1950–2030)

Unit: %

	1950	1980	2000	2010	2020	2030
The South	**28.9**	**24.5**	**29.9**	**41.6**	**50.0**	**60.0**
China	0.9	1.0	3.3	9.1	19.0	27.0
India	1.7	0.7	0.8	2.1	4.5	6.8
Russia			0.7	1.6	2.0	2.5
Brazil	1.7	1.2	0.9	1.2	1.5	1.8
The North	**71.1**	**75.5**	**70.1**	**58.4**	**50.0**	**40.0**
USA	15.0	12.4	18.7	12.8	10.5	9.5
EU			38.4	34.7	30.0	25.0
Japan	1.5	6.8	5.6	4.5	4.0	3.5

Note: The South and the North are defined as in Table 3.3

Sources: Data for 1950–2010 comes from WTO, International Trade Statistics; data for 2020–2030 are the estimates of the author

Table 3.7 World total FDI flow volume percentages for the South and the North (1970–2030)

Unit: %

	1970	1980	1990	2000	2009	2020	2030
The South	**28.9**	**13.9**	**16.9**	**18.8**	**49.2**	**60.0**	**75.0**
China	0.0	0.1	1.7	2.9	8.5	15.0	20.0
The North	**71.1**	**86.1**	**83.1**	**81.2**	**50.8**	**40.0**	**25.0**
North America Free Trade Zone	25.4	45.9	28.2	28.5	14.5	10.0	10.0
EU	38.6	39.4	46.9	49.8	32.5	15.0	18.0

Note: The South and the North are defined as in Table 3.3
Sources: UNCTAD Stat; data for 2020 and 2030 are the estimates of the author

International capital will mainly flow into the South. From 2010 to 2030, the South will become the main destination for foreign direct investments. By 2030, 75% of foreign direct investment will flow into the South (compared with approximately 20% in 2000) (see Table 3.7). The South will become attractive to foreign direct investment because their labor and production factors costs are lower than in the North. In addition, the South will see their levels of economic development improve, as will their average annual incomes. In addition, market demand and market size will continue to expand and their investment conditions will also improve.

In terms of FDI reserve, the North will still occupy a dominant position but the South will be closing the gap. By 2030, the FDI reserve of the South will reach 40% of the world's total while that of China will reach 8.0%.

The FDI outflow of emerging economies (i.e., BRIC countries) will significantly increase; in 2008 it reached US$147 billion, accounting for 9% of the global FDI outflow. Only 10 years earlier, it had measured 1% (UNCTAD 2010). This value will continue to increase.

China will become the biggest foreign direct investor in the world. From 2002 to 2009, China's annual contribution to global FDI inflow was 3%, with a global FDI outflow of 5.5%. In recent years, China's foreign direct investment has increased by more than eight times, from 0.5% in 2002 to 44% in 2009. China has become the fifth largest foreign direct investor. If calculated using a low GDP percentage of 5%, China's FDI will increase by one trillion dollars by 2020. If the percentage rises to the level of 15% like transitional economies, then the Chinese foreign direct investment will reach approximately US$3 trillion a year (Rosen and Hanemann 2011). We estimate that by 2030, China will become the world's No. 1 foreign investor, with its outbound direct investment reaching approximately US$4.5–5 trillion. China's outbound investment includes both China's interests overseas and the huge business opportunities and investment interests China provides to the world. In the future, China's GNP will exceed its GDP. However, international investment in China will continue while the era of China's international investments continues.

Table 3.8 Number of full-time scientists and engineers worldwide and in key countries engaging in R&D (1980–2030)

Unit: millions

	1980	1985	1990	1995	2000	2005	2007	2020	2030
China	0.32	0.34	0.35	0.55	0.69	1.11	1.42	3.00	4.50
USA	0.65	0.80	9.24	0.99	1.26	1.36	1.43	1.80	2.20
EU				1.06	1.09	1.29	1.45	1.80	2.30
Japan	0.63	0.76	0.91	0.99	1.05	1.01	1.05	1.20	1.50
Russia				0.56	0.51	0.47	0.47	0.60	0.80
World				5.38	6.88	8.23	7.21	10.00	15.00

Sources: (1) 1980–1990 data for China was sourced from 40 years of Chinese Science and Technology, China Statistical Press; (2) 1995 and 2000 data are based on the number of researchers per million people from the World Bank's World Development Indicator 2010; (3) 1980–1990 data for the US was sourced from NSF, National Patterns of R&D Resources, 1994; (4) 1980–1990 data for Japan was sourced from Historical Statistics of Japan; (5) 2007 data was sourced from UNESCO, Science, Technology and Gender: An International Report; 2020–2030 data are the estimates of the author; a detailed analysis can be found in section "A strong power in knowledgeable and skilled people" in Chap. 5

Global S&T Revolution and Competition in Innovations

Innovative capacity is a key factor deciding the success or failure of a country in international competition. During the next 20 years, the world will enter into an active period of S&T innovations, representing both the output of scientific research and technological achievements, and the prosperity of the science and technology market, and irrespective of the input capacity of the various countries. All countries will enjoy rapid development during this period. The entire world will herald in a new S&T revolution and fiercer competition in innovations. Historical experience shows that global economic crises often give rise to major S&T innovations and revolutions (Zhang Ping 2011). After the world economy recovers from a short period of crisis, numerous frontier scientific and technological designs are applied in production, which will further increase total labor productivity. At the same time, major breakthroughs are expected in top-end sciences such as biology, materials, space, and energy.

As a result of exceptional activity in global S&T innovation, the output and publication of research papers will maintain its high-speed growth. It is expected that by 2020, the number of S&T papers published annually will reach 1.67 million and the number of international patent applications will reach 1.47 million. By 2030, they will reach 2.31 million and 1.97 million, respectively.

In terms of the development trend in S&T innovation, the gap between the South and the North will be far larger than the disparity in economic development; the speed of convergence will be far greater than that of their economic convergence. The South, represented by China, will become the new innovator and ultimately the main innovator.

Table 3.9 Global R&D input and its share in GDP (1981–2030)

Year	R&D input (100 million dollars)	Share in GDP (%)
1981	5,242	2.0
1990	5,545	1.5
2000	10,310	2.2
2009	11,601	1.8
2020	17,842	2.0
2030	35,968	3.0

Note: Calculated using 2000 PPP

Sources: Data for China were sourced from State Statistical Bureau, Statistical Data Collection for the 60 Years of the New China, China Statistical Yearbook 2010; 1981–1990 data for the USA, Japan, and Russia were sourced from the OECD, OECD Factbook 2005; 1995–2005 data were sourced from the OECD, OECD Factbook 2010; 1981–1990 data for Russia were sourced from the former Soviet Union, from NSF, Science and Engineering Indicators 2000; 1995–2009 data for the EU were sourced from Eurostat, European Commission; 2009 data for the USA and Russia are the same as 2008 data, sourced from NSF, Science and Engineering Indicators 2010; 2009 data for Japan were sourced from Survey of Research & Development, Japan Statistics Bureau & Statistics Center; 2020 and 2030 data are the estimates of the author

The reserve of human capital in science and technology will increase, with top-level science and technical personnel becoming the major force in S&T innovations. The number of full-time scientists and engineers engaging in R&D is likely to reach 15 million worldwide, doubling that of the 2010 level. The total number of scientists and technical personnel in China, the United States, the EU, Japan, and Russia will reach 11.30 million, 75% of the world's total. China will boast the largest number of scientific and technological personnel in the world with 4.5 million, or 30% of the world's total or the combined total of the United States and the EU (see Table 3.8). More frequently, these new and vital forces in the fields of science and technology will come from developing countries. It is also necessary to point out that people in R&D do not only include full-time scientists and engineers but also part-time personnel. In 2010, 2.52 million people were engaged in research and projects; if converted to full-time personnel, the number would be approximately 1.2–1.3 times the number of actual full-time personnel.

Global input in R&D will also significantly increase. According to the 2020 goal set by the EU, and China's aim to invest in medium- and long-term development R&D programs,[12] the input into global science and technology by 2030 is conservatively estimated to be close to US$3.6 trillion, 3% of global GDP, far exceeding the input levels for 2009. The proportion of input in S&T innovations by the United States, the EU, China, and Japan will steadily increase, with that for 2020 and 2030 expected to account for 85 and 93%, respectively, of the world's total (Table 3.9).

The unprecedented future activity of the S&T market, the trading and application of research achievements, and the production and trading of high-tech products will

---

[12] The EU's "2020 Development Goal" and China's State Medium- and Long-term Science and Technology Development Program have both set a goal for science and technology inputs to represent 2% of GDP.

become the main driving forces behind the steady growth of the global economy and will ensure sustainable economic and social development. The percentage of high-tech products in manufactured export goods will increase from 17.3% in 2008 to 24% by 2020, and will reach 30% by 2030.[13] In terms of spatial distribution, China overtook the EU in 2006 to become the world's largest high-tech product exporter, with its exports accounting for 16.9% of the world total in that year; the United States, EU, and Japan held 16.8, 15.0, and 8.0% of the market, respectively (Meri 2009). This development trend will continue into 2030. China's current advantages in high-tech exports will increase. India is also expected to move from behind in the high-tech service trade; with its information technology and accompanying services, India will occupy a strong position in the new international order of science and technology.

In terms of its growth period, the S&T revolution differs from the first and second golden ages of economic growth. First, with regard to the main subjects of innovation, very few countries participated in the two previous golden ages. In contrast, in the current S&T revolution, the number of participating countries will increase significantly. Second, in the past, the sharing, diffusion, and application of achievements were confined to a limited number of countries. Now these successes will spread to a greater number of countries. The current scope of ICT application is obviously greater than that of the electrical revolution of the first golden age. Third, technology inventions will concentrate on a number of technologies, including health, ICT, biology, and new energy sources, and this will quickly become commercialized.

Period of Global Population Aging and Urbanization Acceleration

The global trend of population development has experienced irreversible changes in both its spatial distribution and population structure. In terms of labor supply and total employment, more and more people have participated in the process of globalization and supported the prosperity of the world economy, assuming a scale far larger than that of the second golden period.

The global population will continue to grow to reach 8.32 billion by 2030, 1.42 billion more than in 2010. From 2010 to 2030, the natural growth rate of the global population and the total fertility rate of women will assume a downward trend. The natural growth rate will drop from 22.4% in 2010 to 16.2%, and the total fertility rate of women worldwide will drop from 2.79 in 2010 to 2.29 by 2030. The most populous country, China, will reach its peak of 1.395 billion in total population at around 2025. India is likely to overtake China to become the No. 1 country in terms of total population by 2024–2025.

---

[13] 1980–2008 data was sourced from the World Bank, World Development Indicator 2010; 2020 and 2030 data are the calculations of the author.

Table 3.10 World total working age population percentages for the South and the North (1950–2030)

Unit: %

	1950	1970	1990	2000	2010	2020	2030
The South	**74.6**	**77.4**	**81.9**	**83.8**	**85.4**	**86.8**	**88.0**
Developing Asian countries	50.4	52.0	56.8	58.1	59.2	59.4	58.6
China	22.0	21.7	23.3	22.2	21.4	19.7	17.7
India	14.4	14.6	15.7	16.7	17.5	18.3	19.0
Russia	4.3	4.1	3.1	2.6	2.3	1.9	1.6
Brazil	2.0	2.5	2.8	2.9	2.9	2.9	2.8
The North	**25.4**	**22.6**	**18.1**	**16.2**	**14.6**	**13.2**	**12.0**
USA	6.7	6.1	5.1	4.9	4.6	4.3	4.1
EU	13.1	10.8	8.0	6.9	6.2	5.5	4.9
Japan	3.2	3.4	2.6	2.2	1.8	1.5	1.3

Note: Working age population refers to people aged between 15 and 64 years old; The South and the North, and developing Asian countries are defined as in Table 3.3
Sources: Population Division of the Department of Economic and Social Affairs of the United Nations Secretariat, World Population Prospects: The 2010 Revision, http://esa.un.org/unpd/wpp/index.htm

The global population structure will be an aging population and characterized by fewer children. The middle age of the global population will increase from 29.2 years in 2010 to 34.1 years by 2030, with those aged above 65 years accounting for 11.7% of the population by 2030, compared with 7.6% in 2010, indicating a typical aging society. The percentage of the population aged 0–14 will decrease from 26.8% in 2010 to 22.9% by 2030. As India, Indonesia, Brazil, and the majority of African countries enjoy population dividends, the percentage of the working population in these countries will increase, thus keeping the percentage of the total global working age population basically stable, and at a higher level than in the latter half of the previous century. The population dependency rate will be kept fairly low for some time yet (see Table 3.10).[14]

The global population structure will assume a significant trend in a shift from rural to urban, increasing the rate of global urbanization, which will reach 59% by 2030. At that time, the South will hold 81.8% of the urban population, while the North will be home to less than 20% (see Table 3.11). Although the urbanization rate is likely to slow, the annual average growth of the urban population will top 1%. In this process, the cluster effect of urbanization will become more obvious. A higher urbanization means a bigger consumer market, especially in the South, which will become a leading player in the growth of global consumption. By 2025, two billion people, or 25% of the global population, will live in the world's 600 largest cities. These cities will create US$64 trillion in GDP, close to 60% of

[14] By 2030, the overwhelming majority of African countries will see their populations aged 30 years and under exceed 60% and the share of the population aged 30 years and under will be 45–59% in southern and western Asia (excluding Iran, South America, Argentina, Uruguay, and Chile).

Table 3.11 World total population percentages for the South and the North (1950–2030)

Unit: %

	1950	1970	1990	2000	2010	2020	2030
The South	**52.4**	**61.5**	**71.7**	**75.1**	**77.6**	**79.8**	**81.8**
Developing Asian countries	26.5	30.7	39.2	43.3	46.4	48.5	50.1
China	8.8	10.7	13.4	16.0	19.1	21.0	22.9
India	8.7	8.2	9.8	10.2	10.5	11.1	12.0
Russia	6.2	6.1	4.8	3.8	2.9	2.4	2.0
Brazil	2.7	4.0	4.9	5.0	4.9	4.5	4.0
The North	**47.6**	**38.5**	**28.3**	**24.9**	**22.4**	**20.2**	**18.2**
USA	13.9	11.6	8.5	8.0	7.5	7.0	6.6
EU	21.5	16.1	11.2	9.2	8.2	7.3	6.5
Japan	4.0	4.2	3.4	2.9	2.4	2.1	1.7
China/USA							3.5

Note: The South and the North are defined as in Table 3.3

Sources: Population Division of the Department of Economic and Social Affairs of the United Nations Secretariat, World Population Prospects: The 2010 Revision, http://esa.un.org/unpd/wpp/index.htm; data for China was sourced from national population census from various years.

global GDP. There will be 735 million families with an average annual income per person of US\$32,000 in the 600 largest cities. Of these, 235 million families will be living in developing countries, with their per capita annual income at more than US\$20,000 (McKinsey Global Institute report 2011). However, city slums are likely to become a factor influencing the quality of urbanization development. This is a glaring problem facing the governments of all countries as they push their strategies for urbanization.

Global Green Revolution and Green Energy

The global primary energy demand and consumption structure will experience a period of adjustment, starting with a transition to green energy sources.[15] According to a prediction by the International Energy Agency, coal consumption will increase from 22.9% in 2000 to 29.1% by 2030; petroleum consumption will reduce from 36.5% in 2000 to 29.8% by 2030. Renewable energy sources such as nuclear energy, water energy, and biological energy are expected to remain stable. During this period, all countries will be dedicated to developing green energy, and to the R&D of new energy technologies such as wind energy, solar energy, and bio-energy. By 2030, the world will enter a crucial transition period regarding energy consumption. The production of global liquid hydrocarbon (such as petroleum and liquefied natural gas) will begin to decline. By that stage, it will be difficult to predict whether new energy technologies will be able to replace traditional energies (National Intelligence Council 2008).

---

[15] Green energy has three meanings: cleaning of traditional energy, renewable energy, and the highly efficient use of energy.

Table 3.12 World total percentages of the primary energy demands of the South and the North (1980–2030)

Unit: %

	1980	2000	2007	2015	2020	2030
The South	**44.0**	**47.6**	**54.2**	**59.5**	**62.1**	**65.4**
China	8.3	11.0	16.4	20.6	22.1	22.8
India	2.9	4.6	5.0	5.7	6.2	7.7
Latin America	4.0	4.6	4.6	4.7	4.7	4.9
The North	**56.0**	**52.4**	**45.8**	**40.5**	**37.9**	**34.6**
USA	24.9	22.8	19.5	17.0	15.8	14.3
EU		16.8	14.6	12.7	11.8	10.6
Japan	4.8	5.2	4.3	3.6	3.3	2.9

Notes: The South, the North, and developing countries are defined as in Table 3.3
Sources: International Energy Agency, World Energy Outlook 2009, 2001; data for 2020–2030 are estimates based on an IEA model

The South will quickly become the main consumer of primary energy, with China taking the first position. The North will consume 34.6% of primary energy sources, compared with 56% in 1980. The South's primary energy consumption will jump from 44 to 65.4%. By 2030 China's primary energy demand will reach 22.8% of the world's total, equal to those of the United States and the EU combined (see Table 3.12).

Climate change will become a common challenge for all countries. Global carbon emissions are likely to peak between 2020 and 2030. IEA predictions shows that it is likely to peak sometime between 2020 and 2030 if all countries cooperate in the launching of an energy and environmental revolution. Carbon emissions will drop sharply after that time, when global economic development is expected to reduce carbon emissions.[16]

The green industrial revolution will become the goal of the world. At its core is the desire to fundamentally change the worldwide economic development model and roadmap that has been in place since 1750. In the twenty-first century, China will face its most important strategic opportunity to become an active participant of this green revolution and a leader of innovation. China will initiate innovative green action and implement green development strategies—it will synchronize its step with that of the rest of the world. China will strive to bring about the peak of carbon emissions sometime in 2020–2050, and then its sharp decline.

---

[16] If the atmosphere's global hothouse gas density is stabilized at 450 ppm CO_2 equivalent (the so-called "450 scenario"), then global CO_2 emissions will peak at 30.7 billion tons (carbon equivalent) by 2020, CO_2 emissions will drop to 24–26 billion tons (carbon equivalent) by 2030, and to 10 billion tons (carbon equivalent) by 2050, about half that of 1990 (20.9 billion tons, carbon equivalent) (International Energy Agency 2011b).

Brief Summary: Toward a World of Common Prosperity

The shift toward a harmonious world is one of China's key objectives, which stem from China's traditional theories on governance. Furthermore, the realization of common prosperity represents the perfect expression of this objective. To promote worldwide common wealth and common prosperity is the external expression of great harmony.

Common prosperity has the following meanings: first, to reduce the poverty rate; second, to increase per capita income; and third, to increase human development levels. The world is clearly moving in this direction, and over the next 20 years the major structural indices of the South and the North will begin to converge; we will see the South wind overwhelming the North wind.

There are signs that the world is beginning to realize the value of common wealth and common prosperity. They are seen in the shift from the North to the South of the processes of global economic resources, innovative resources and human resources. Global wealth represents the convergence per capita income levels for all countries; global prosperity refers to the collective increase of human development, ultimately to a level of convergence.

The nearly 200 years of modern economic growth represents an era of "great divergence"[17] with the north-south gap constantly growing wider. It is a history of inequity, injustice, and unfairness, with the North dominating the world economic order.

The sustained high growth of China and India with populations of billions could stimulate a shift from the "great divergence era," which lasted for two centuries, to the "great convergence era" of the twenty-first century,[18] although the inequity co-efficients among countries will still be high.

We hold that in the following 20 years, the world will enter into an era of "great convergence," largely because of the independent development experienced by the

---

[17] Since 1820, while the world's per capita GDP has been growing, the long-term trend has been a growing disparity in income. According to calculations and analysis by Angus Maddison, this manifests itself in a disparity among the various larger regions, which was less than 3:1 in 1820, but reached 16:1 in 1992. It is also manifested in the gap among different countries (between dominant countries and the countries with the poorest performances), which exceeded 3:1 in 1820 but reached 72:1 in 1992. Only a small group of lagging countries caught up after World War II and convergence occurred (see Maddison 1995). After World War II, per capita GDP in the South reduced compared with the per capita GDP of the North, from 20.5% in 1950 to 17.1% by 1970, and tp 13.5% by 2000. Per capita GDP in developing Asian countries reduced from 11.8% in 1950 to 10.0% by 1970, but increased to 13.5% by 2000, thanks to the economic take-off of the Asia's Four Little Dragons, China, India, and Southeast Asia.

[18] According to the calculations of the World Bank, since 1950, the weighted inequality (Gini Co-efficient) has been in a continuous decline, mainly because income has been growing in population-dense countries such as China and India. However, if China and India are excluded, international inequality (Gini Co-efficient) increased after the 1980s. Since 1950, the un-weighted country inequality (Gini Co-efficient) has assumed a long-term upward trend. However, in the recent period, especially in the 1990s, international inequality was reduced, mainly because of an increase in the income of China and South Asia (see The World Bank 2006).

Table 3.13 Catching-up co-efficients of per capita GDP for the South vs. the North (1950–2030)

	1950	1970	2000	2010	2020	2030
The South	**20.5**	**17.1**	**13.5**	**18.1**	**24.1**	**34.4**
Developing Asian countries	11.8	10.0	13.5	21.0	29.6	44.4
China	8.3	7.1	15.2	31.5	55.0	85.7
India	11.3	7.0	8.1	13.3	23.2	43.6

Note: The North = 100 countries
Sources: Angus Maddison, 2010, Population Division of the Department of Economic and Social Affairs of the United Nations Secretariat, World Population Prospects: The 2010 Revision, http:// esa.un.org/unpd/wpp/index.htm; data for 2020 and 2030 are the estimates of the author

South. International inequity will be reduced in many areas, including education,[19] health,[20] and in other social indicators. In addition, per capita GDP and per capita income will also be reduced. The South and the North will converge in terms of education and health, driven by a globalization of knowledge and politics, economy and education.

In the following 20 years, the income levels of all countries will converge. In 2010, the per capita GDP of the South was, by and large, one-sixth the average of the North. However, with the rapid development of the South, their per capita GDP is expected to reach one-third that of the North by 2030. The income gaps between the two groups will quickly narrow, with the per capita GDP catching-up indices of the two biggest countries in the South, China and India, likely to reach 85.7 and 43.6% of the North, respectively (see Table 3.13). China and India's economic growth will arrest the worsening situation of income inequity (The World Bank 2006).

The world as a whole is likely to enter a stage of high human development. According to a new computation method developed by UNDP, China's human development index (HDI) was 0.663 in 2010 (an upper-middle level ranking) while the world's HDI was 0.624 (a lower-middle level ranking). By 2020, global HDI will be at 0.696, close to high levels, while China's HDI will be 0.750, well within the high level.

In terms of the composition of HDI, global per capita GDP will reach US$14,000 by 2020; the average years of education received will reach 8 years; the expected years of education will be at 13 years; and the expected mean life expectancy will equal 75 years. These four indicators for China will be US$14,000, 10 years, 14 years, and 77.5 years, respectively. By 2030, global HDI will be 0.703, recognized as a high level, while China's HDI will be 0.776 and is likely to exceed 0.800 between 2040 and 2050. In terms of HDI indicators, by 2030 global per capita GDP will reach US$19,000; the average years of education received will equal 9.5 years;

---

[19] According to calculations of the World Bank, the global average years of education received increased from 3.4 years to 6.3 years in 2000, while the education inequity variant co-efficient dropped from 0.739 to 0.461 (see The World Bank 2006).

[20] According to a study by the World Bank, while the world's mean life expectancy has increased, the inequity in the mean life expectancy among the countries has been reduced, with the variant co-efficient declining from 0.233 in 1960 to 0.194 in 2000 (see The World Bank 2006).

Table 3.14 International poverty occurrence rate in China, India, and other developing countries (1990–2030)

Unit: %

	1990	2005	2015	2020	2030
China	60.2	15.9	<5	1	
India	51.3	41.6	22	15	<10
Other Developing countries	46.0	27.0	<15	<10	<5

Note: The international poverty occurrence rate is calculated according to the international absolute poverty line (1.25 dollars per person per day)
Data sources: UN, Millennium Development Goal Report 2011; China Statistical Abstract 2011; World Bank, World Development Indicator 2011; 2020 and 2030 data are estimates of the author

expected years of education received will be at 14 years; and the mean life expectancy will be 79 years. These four indicators for China will be US$23,000, 10 years, 16 years, and 80 years, respectively.

The millennium development goal (MDG) and the international governance system under the direction of the MDG will effectively push for global human development and greatly reduce the percentage of poverty-stricken people.[21] The number of people in developing countries living below the international absolute poverty line (1.25 dollars per person per day) was reduced from 1.8 billion in 1990 to 1.4 billion in 2005, with the relative poverty rate lowered from 46 to 27%. By 2015, the total poverty occurrence rate is expected to drop to below 15% (UN 2011). Under this trend, the poverty occurrence rate in developing countries will drop to below 10% by 2020 and then to below 5% by 2030 (see Table 3.14); thus, basically eliminating international absolute poverty. Therefore, the United Nations and the international community will have to formulate a further MDG for the second stage (2015–2030). With the close cooperation of all governments and the action of an effective international governance mechanism, we may well see the realization of this dream.

China has made and will continue to make worldwide contributions to achieve global common wealth and common prosperity, and it will undertake even greater responsibilities. The rise of China benefits the world as a whole. However, such development also represents greater expectations and responsibilities.[22] The rapid rise of China has not only changed the pattern of trial of strength but also the role

---

[21] The United Nations put forward a global MDG in 2000 for the purpose of eradicating absolute poverty and improving the standard of living of developing countries. According to the MDG Goal Report released in 2011, if the governments of all countries commit to the specific measures and steps, then the MDG will be realized. Thus, it is expected that the global elimination of extreme poverty and hunger can be achieved by 2015, in addition to compulsory primary school education, promoting gender equality and empowering women, a reduction in the child mortality rate, improving the health of pregnant women, and fighting AIDS, malaria and other diseases, and ensuring the sustainability of the environment. Worldwide, people will enjoy more equitable development opportunities and fully enjoy the dividends of global economic integration.

[22] Ban Ki-moon, Let China be the country to show the way ahead, Speech at Nanjing University, October 31, 2010.

of China within the international system. This has created unrivaled historical development opportunities for China.

Within the context of profound change and daily development changes, only by having an overall and profound knowledge of the world situation, is it possible for us to obtain an accurate picture of China; only by acutely discerning, and in a forward-looking manner, the new trends and characteristics of world development, is it possible for us to be more active in creating strategic opportunities and to preempt the heights of the various international revolutions (industrial, energy, science and technology, and knowledge); only by obtaining a better command of both domestic

---

Box 3.2 Common Efforts to Build a World of Great Harmony

A peaceful world. The twenty-first century is characteristically a peaceful century. All countries need a peaceful environment to enable significant development. It is in the public interest to prevent a further world war and war among the key powers. For developing countries, peace is also the greatest public good. By safeguarding world peace, China is providing the world with the greatest and most important public good.[23] We are spreading the idea of peaceful development and this will further promote a peaceful environment for China and the rest of the world. Peace will enable strategic development opportunities and favorable external conditions.

A harmonious world. It is necessary to end the current unequal and unjust international order. The rapid rise of the South has changed the trial-of-strength pattern and stimulated the reform and readjustment of the global governance system. In addition, it has broken the order that has long been monopolized by the United States and has won a greater voice for developing countries. The rise of the South has broken the monopoly and exclusiveness enjoyed by Western cultures and has introduced a more diversified international culture and values.

A world of common wealth. It is necessary to encourage the values of globalism; it is necessary to promote common development, helping the South to accelerate its development and to narrow the South-North gaps. The keyword here is common. The essence of which is the internationalization of China's concept of common wealth. This will lead to mutually beneficial acts of cooperation to build a more just and equal global governance structure. The keyword is here is mutual, which is the polar opposite of the Western capitalist practice of "harming others to benefit their own."

(continued)

---

[23] In 1987, Deng Xiaoping put forward his "70-year theory," that is, China requires a long period of peaceful international, from 1980 to 2050, so as to realize its three-step strategy. Deng Xiaoping said that China can realize the goal of ending poverty and attaining a comfortable living by the end of this century. But to reach the levels of mid-developed countries, will take about 50 years. Thus, we hope that there will be at least 70 years of peace. We must lose this period (Deng Xiaoping 1993b).

Box 3.2 (continued)

A green world. It is necessary to make common efforts to bring about the "fourth industrial revolution" (a green industrial revolution), to create a new green development model, to develop a low-carbon economy, and become involved in international negotiations and the formulation of international rules for managing climate change.

and international situations and better implementing the two major national policies of expanding domestic demand and opening across-the-board, is it possible for us to realize the goal of building a well-rounded and prosperous society, and the great rejuvenation of the nation of China.

Despite the existing and increasing uncertainties in the international environment, China's external environment and favorable conditions have not fundamentally changed. The international environment regarding the economy, science and technology, politics, and security is at its strongest since the founding of the New China. China has been endowed with the historical opportunities of peaceful development.

Contemporary China is experiencing unprecedented economic development, social transition, and social change. The contemporary world is experiencing unprecedented development, changes, and adjustment. Peace, development, and cooperation are now mainstream, and have created favorable conditions for common efforts to build a world of great harmony (see Box 3.2). For China, a foremost objective is to safeguard world peace and prevent any further world wars, and to prevent wars among the world powers so as to maintain an internationally peaceful environment for the following 20 years (or longer). It is then necessary to promote common development, to help the South to accelerate the speed of their development and to narrow the various South-North gaps. Such measures will help to achieve the internationalization and globalization of common wealth. It is necessary to strengthen mutually beneficial cooperation in order to establish a fairer and more just global governance structure; the key word here is mutual. It is essential to change the current unfair, unjust, and unequal practices. Peace is the basic condition for development; cooperation is the basic channel for promoting development; and development is the basic goal of peace and cooperation (see Box 3.2).

References

Barro RJ, Jong-Wha Lee (2010) A new data set of educational attainment in the world, 1950–2010, NBER working paper No. 15902. NBER, Cambridge

Deng Xiaoping (1993a) Establishing a new international order according to the five principles of peaceful co-existence. In: Selected works of Deng Xiaoping. People's Publishing House, Beijing, p 282

Deng Xiaoping (1993b) Two basic points for our principles and policies. In: Selected works of Deng Xiaoping, vol 3. Beijing People's Publishing House, Beijing, p 250, July 4, 1987

Fogel R (2007) Capitalism and democracy in 2040: forecasts and speculations, NBER working paper no. 13184. NBER, Cambridge

Fogel R (2008) The impact of the Asian miracle on the theory of economic growth, Working paper, Chicago

International Energy Agency (2011a) World energy outlook 2009. International Energy Agency, Paris, p 185

International Energy Agency (2011b) World energy outlook 2009. International Energy Agency, Paris, p 172

Jiang Zemin (2002) Building a well-off society and break new ground in creating a new situation for the cause of socialism with Chinese characteristics—report to the 16th National Party Congress, Beijing, 8 Nov 2002

Maddison A (1995) Monitoring the world economy 1820–1992. OECD Development Center, Paris

Maddison A (2001) The world economy: a millennial perspective. OECD Development Centre, Paris

Maddison A (2003) Millennium history of the world economy. Beijing University Press, Beijing, pp 115–116, November

Maddison A (2008) Long-term performance of the Chinese economy: 1960–2030. Shanghai People's Publishing House, Shanghai, p 106, March

McKinsey Global Institute (2011) Urban world: mapping the economic power of cities (McKinsey Global Institute report). McKinsey Global Institute, New York, p 5

Meri T (2009) China Passes the EU in High-tech Exports, EuroStat Statistics in Focus, No. 25/2009

National Intelligence Council (2008) Global trends 2025: a transformed world. National Intelligence Council, Washington, DC, p 25

Rosen DH, Hanemann T (2011) An American open door? Maximizing the Benefits of Chinese Foreign Direct Investment. Center on U.S.-China Relations Asia Society and Kissinger Institute on China and the United States, Woodrow Wilson International Center for Scholars Special report, May 2011

The World Bank (2006) World development report 2006: equity and development, Chinese edition. Tsinghua University Press, Beijing, pp 62–63

UN (2011) Millennium development goal report 2011. United Nations, New York, pp 6–7, July 7

UNCTAD (2010) World investment report 2010: investing in a low-carbon economy. United Nations, Geneva, p 7

Zhang Ping (ed) (Apr 2011) Guide to the reader of the 12th five-year program for economic and social development of the people's republic of China. People's Publishing House, Beijing, p 38

Chapter 4
World Economic Power

Once built up, China will be a great socialist country ...
it will be able to catch up with the most powerful capitalist
country in the world, the United States.

Mao Zedong (1956)

The New China of the 1950s, not long after it was founded, was a backward, despised and wretched country. It was one of the poorest and most undeveloped countries in the world. It was at that time that Mao Zedong proudly told the delegates of the 8th National Party Congress:

> ... it will be able to catch up with the most powerful capitalist country in the world, the United States. (This was 200 years after the US was founded—author.) The United States has a population of only 170 million, and as we have a population several times larger, are similarly rich in resources and are favored with more or less the same kind of climate, it is possible for us to catch up with the United States. Oughtn't we to catch up? Definitely yes ... Given fifty (2006—author) or sixty years (i.e., 2016—author), we certainly ought to overtake the United States.

Mao Zedong stated that it was important that China surpass the United States; "you are said to be building socialism, which is supposed to be superior"(Mao Zedong 1977).

The prophetic powers of Mao Zedong have been repeatedly proven by history. When Mao made these comments he was not aware of GDP; he was referring to China's steel output. In 1955, the United States' crude steel output topped 100 million tons (106.17 million tons), 37.2 times that of China (2.853 million tons). However, by 1993, China had overtaken the United States (Japanese Society for the Study of National Conditions 2011). By 2010, the United States' crude steel output was 88.475 million tons compared with China's 626.96 million tons, which was seven

A. Hu et al., *China 2030*, DOI 10.1007/978-3-642-31328-8_4,
© Springer-Verlag Berlin Heidelberg 2014

times greater. If compared in GDP terms, China overtook Japan in 2010, ranking second in the world (Ma Jiantang 2011). If calculated using exchange rate and PPP, China will overtake the United State in GDP aggregate before 2020 and by 2030, China's GDP aggregate will be 2.0–2.2 times that of the United States.

By 2030, China will overtake the United States to become the biggest economy in the world, with the largest consumer market, the largest modern industrial system, the largest city groups, and the largest, most modern infrastructure system. This will determine China's status and role in the future world order, which will directly stimulate economic development, social progress, and the economic integration of the South.

Of course, China will also face many new challenges over the next 20 years, including resources, environment, an extensive trade model, low-employment growth model, irrational income distribution, excessive bank savings, industry-dominated development (heavy industry), low birth rates, and an aging population.[1] Although China may lose some of its traditional comparative advantages, we believe that the driving factors, market conditions, institutional advantages, and other influencing factors will remain unchanged and high-speed growth will be maintained. Furthermore, new competitive advantages (human capital accumulation and innovation drive) may also emerge. China will create new and greater "miracles." Our prediction will be proven correct over time.

World's Largest Economy

In 1984, when China began to open its door to the world, it was both a vast economic power, and one of the poorest countries in the world. Deng Xiaoping, the architect of the reform and subsequent opening up, explained, "The superiority of socialism lies in the fact that its productivity develops higher and faster than that of capitalism" (Deng Xiaoping 1986).

Since reform and opening up, China has made full use of the many functions of the invisible hand of the market to create wealth, and has applied the full extent of the visible hand of the government through plan guidance during the transition period to a socialist market economy.

Nobel laureate in Economics, Michael Spence offered high praise regarding China's economic growth since the reform and opening up, commenting that, "Among all the cases that have realized high-speed growth, China's growth is the biggest and the fastest. Such speed and scale of growth is unprecedented" (Spence 2008).

China has created an economic miracle on a scale that is the largest and fastest in history. China has maintained its strong and rapid growth for more than 30 years. Its average annual GDP growth was as high as 9.89% from 1978 to 2010, with the

---

[1] We have discussed these problems thoroughly. For a detailed analysis and key data, see the China Study Center, Tsinghua University (Angang Hu and Wu Yilong 2010).

2010 rate 20.57 times that of 1978 (China State Statistical Bureau 2011). In the 30 years from 1978 to 2008, China's growth was one of the fastest (of the 166 countries with GDP statistics), with a growth rate of 9.8%, 3 percentage points higher than Singapore, which was ranked second. This round of high-speed development enabled China to significantly bridge the existing gaps with developed Western countries and to further widen the gaps with India and other countries.[2] In the same period, China was the most stable country in the world, with a GDP fluctuation co-efficient of 0.28, the smallest among the 20 fastest growing economies.[3]

During the next 20 years, China will remain in an economic "takeoff" stage, with its growth still promising great potential and growth momentum, maintaining long-term, high-speed growth. Despite the fact that economic growth has been constrained by resources, environment and climate change, we estimate that China's economy will maintain 7–8% growth from 2011 to 2030.

Between 2011 and 2030, China's GDP potential growth rate could be anywhere from 5.9 to 9.2%,[4] without taking into account ecological constraints. Furthermore, potential GDP growth could be close to 7.9%. When consideration is given to the constraints of energy supply, resource consumption, ecological environment and CO_2 emissions, and the fact that the Chinese government will not pursue its development goals at a cost to everything else, China will instead seek growth quality via a lowered growth rate. An appropriate growth rate for the next 20 years is around 7.5% (8% for 2011–2020 and 7% for 2021–2030). The appropriate growth is largely one percentage point lower than potential growth. Of course, due to the uncertainty principle[5] with regard to GDP, the real growth rate will be within the range of potential growth (Table 4.1).

With 1978 as the base figure and calculated using the constant price method, China's GDP for 2010 has grown 20.57 times (State Statistical Bureau 2011) since 1978, and will have increased by 44.4 times by 2020, and 87.4 times by 2030. Thus, it would be true to say that there will be no other country capable of increasing its economic aggregate by more than 80 times in a mere 52 years. This is double the 40 times growth co-efficient of the GDP growth for the 12 Western European countries in the 172 years from 1820 to 1992 (Angus Maddison 1995). Listed below are a number of factors favorable to growth, which can explain why China will be able to maintain such high-speed growth over the next 20 years.

---

[2] The figure was calculated by the author based on data from the indicator databank of the World Bank.

[3] These figures were calculated by the author based on data from the development indicators databank of the World Bank.

[4] This is close to the prediction by Wang Xiaolu. He predicted that China's economic growth rate would between 6.7 and 9.0 for 2008–2020 (Wang Xiaolu et al. 2009).

[5] The GDP Uncertainty Principle has been developed according to the computation principles of quantum mechanics. That is, in a quantum mechanics system, the position and momentum of a particle cannot be fixed. The definition of GDP is very clear, that is, it is the end result of all the production activities of all resident units of a country for a given period of time calculated by the market price. However, different methods for measuring GDP may yield quite different results.

Table 4.1 Predictions for China's potential GDP growth (2011–2030)

Unit: %

	2011–2015	2016–2020	2021–2025	2026–2030	2011–2030
GDP proper growth	8	8	7	7	7.5
GDP potential growth	8.9	8.5	7.4	6.9	7.9
Range of GDP potential growth	6.9–11.8	6.3–11	5.5–9.5	5–9	5.9–9.2
Labor power growth	0.6	0.2	0.1	0	0.2
Human capital growth	2.5	2	1.5	1.2	1.8
Capital growth	10	10	9	8	9.3
TFP growth	4	3.8	3.3	3.3	3.6

Note: Capital input weight is 0.4, input is 0.3, and human capital input is 0.3; TFP=total factor productivity; the data are the estimates of the author

First, China's domestic bank savings rate and investment rate have been steadily increasing. Capital formation has assumed an upward trend in its share of GDP. Our most conservative estimate is that for 2010–2020, physical capital investments will grow by at least 10% and it will be above 8% for 2020–2030.[6] This is an important source of growth for China's high-speed development.

Second, China has maintained a relatively high level of human capital growth. On entering the twenty-first century, China accelerated its human capital input. We estimate that the human capital input (average years of education received by the population aged 15 years and above) for 2010–2020 will be 2%, and for 2020–2030 it will be between 1.2 and 1.5%.

Third, China's labor input growth will decline, but employment levels in non-agricultural sectors will rapidly increase. With the total population reaching its peak and an aging population, the working age population will enter a zero-growth stage (<0.2%). At the same time, agricultural laborers will move to non-agricultural employment. The steady drop in agricultural labor is also favorable for raising labor productivity. We estimate that by 2015, China's agricultural labor may be reduced to approximately 250 million, and then further 150 million by 2030. The non-agricultural labor force is expected to grow by 2–3% a year on average. This is a sound labor input for non-agricultural areas, which claim the largest share of the economic aggregate.[7]

Fourth, the key to high-speed economic growth lies in the growth of TFP.[8] As there is still a large gap to bridge with regard to reaching the technology levels

---

[6] Wang Xiaolu and others have predicted the rate to be more than 13% (see Wang Xiaolu et al. 2009).

[7] In 2000–2008, labor levels in China's non-agricultural sectors increased from 360.42 million to 468.26 million, averaging an annual growth of 13.5 million or 3.3%.

[8] This point was raised by Angang Hu with Chinese leaders in 2001. His basic conclusion was that in the future the growth of labor and capital will be limited to economic growth. The key factor influencing economic growth is the rise of TFP. China's growth model will be shifted from "quantity" to "quality," that is, economic growth will be centered round quality, not only including the rise of per capita income levels but also including fairer education and employment opportunities,

of the West, China may have to stimulate its technical progress through imports and consumption. China will become an innovative big power and will play a leading role in the green industrial revolution. This will also further stimulate technical progress. At the same time, there is still the opportunity for China to increase its levels of efficiency and technology. We estimate that China's TFP will be 3.6% from 2011 to 2030.

We have constructed a spatial model with potential output and unemployment as unobservable variables to measure TFP and have arrived at similar conclusions (see Appendix 1).

Of course, any method of prediction has its limitations and errors. What is more important is to see the inherent dynamic factors of economic growth. Since the reform and opening up, China has experienced the fastest and largest degree of industrialization, urbanization, information ecology, internationalization, and infrastructure modernization in human history. These are the five major engines for maintaining high-speed growth. In the next 20 years, these growth engines will continue to provide further unceasing motivation for China's economic growth. China will become the world's largest manufacturer as industrialization accelerates; the speed of China's urbanization will also increase to create a country with the world's largest urban population; the accelerated development of China's information and knowledge society will make it the largest worldwide. The accelerated modernization of China's infrastructure will make China the biggest investor and a leader in modern infrastructure (e.g., high-speed railway networks, high-speed road networks, large air transport hubs, super harbors, and super smart grids). Accelerated internationalization will make China the largest exporter and importer, as well as the biggest service provider. These five major engines are interactive, mutually reinforcing and in demand, and mutually promote each other. It is likely that there are no other highly industrialized and modernized regions in the world that have these five engines; for example, the United States, the EU and Japan typically only have one or two economic growth engines. Thus, we believe that the presence of these five engines provides strong confidence for China's long-term economic growth in the future.

With regard to GDP predictions, this book uses three methods to calculate the dollar value of GDP for 2010–2030, and the index that will show China's catch up to and overtaking of the United States in GDP levels (Table 4.2).

The first is the exchange rate method or market exchange rate. After taking into account China's nominal GDP deflator and the changes in the RMB/US$ exchange rate, China's GDP in 2010 was US$5.8 trillion, 40.2% of the GDP of the United States.

---

greater gender equality, better health and nutrition, a more sustainable natural environment, greater justice in the administration of the law and legal system, a more abundant cultural life, and greater efficiency in social governance (see Angang Hu 2001); World Bank experts hold that the driving force behind China's high-speed development is high TFP growth. From 2005 to 2020, its growth rate will be approximately 3.5–4.0%. See Aloysius Kuijs, "China Economic Quarterly", World Bank, September 2007.

Table 4.2 GDP (US$) for China and the United States and coefficient regarding China's catch up with and overtaking of the United States (2000–2030)

		2000	2010	2015	2020	2025	2030
GDP (US$ trillion)							
Exchange rate method	China	1.2	5.8	11.5	22.7	38.8	66.4
(current price)	USA	9.9	14.7	17.9	21.9	26.6	32.5
PPP (current price)	China	3.0	9.8	15.6	24.7	35.7	51.6
(World Bank)	USA	9.9	14.5	16.4	18.5	21.0	23.7
PPP (1990 price)	China	4.3	10.7	15.0	21.1	26.9	34.4
(Maddison)	USA	8.0	9.5	10.7	12.2	13.8	15.6
Catch up coefficient (USA = 100)							
Exchange rate method		12.1	39.6	64.1	103.9	145.7	204.4
(current price)							
PPP (current price)		30.2	67.8	95.2	133.5	170.3	217.4
(World Bank)							
PPP (1990 price)		53.8	112.9	140.0	173.5	195.7	220.8
(Maddison)							

Note: (1) The catch up coefficient refers to the ratio of China's GDP to that of the US, with the US being 100.(2) For GDP calculated using the exchange rate method, China's real GDP growth will be 8% for 2010–2020, with the GDP deflator at 3%, RMB will appreciate at 3%; the real growth of GDP for the United States will be 2%, with the GDP deflator at 2%. Between 2020 and 2030, the growth of China's gap in real terms will be 7%, with the GDP deflator at 2%; the value of RMB to the dollar will rise by 2%; the real growth of GDP for the United States will be 2%, with the GDP deflator at 2%. (3) As to GDP calculated using the PPP current price method, the GDP deflator will be at 2.5% for 2010–2030. (4) As to GDP calculated using the PPP constant price method, the real growth of China's GDP will be 7% for 2010–2020, 5% for 2020–2030, and that of the United States will be 2.5% for 2010–2030
Sources: World Bank, World Development Indicator 2011; Angus Maddison, Statistics on World Population, GDP and Per Capita GDP, 1–2008 AD, 2010, http://www.ggdc.net/MADDISON/oriindex.htm

By 2019, it will reach US$19.8 trillion, overtaking the United States (US$18.9 trillion), and then by 2030, China's GDP will reach US$66.4 trillion, 2.5 times that of the United States.

The second is the PPP current price method upheld by the World Bank. By this method, China's 2010 GDP is US$9.8 trillion, 67.8% that of the United States. As of 2020, it will reach US$17.1 trillion, overtaking the United States (US$16.8 trillion), and by 2030, China's GDP will reach US$51.6 trillion, 2.2 times that of the United States.

The third method is Maddison's PPP constant price method. By this method, China's 2010 GDP is US$10.7 trillion, 1.1 times that of the United States. As of 2020, it will reach US$21.1 trillion, 1.7 times that of the United States, and by 2030, China's GDP will reach US$34.4 trillion, 2.2 times that of the United States.

No matter what method is used, the results are similar. China's economic aggregate was between 12 and 54% of the United States rate for 2000; by 2010, China's GDP was 0.4–1.1 times that of the United States; before 2020, China will overtake the United States in GDP (with a GDP 1.04–1.74 times greater than that of the United States). Between 2020 and 2030, China's GDP will be 2.2–2.5 times that of the United States (Table 4.2).

Table 4.3 Expenditure components within China's GDP (2000–2030)

Unit: %

	2000	2010	2015	2020	2025	2030
Investments	35.3	48.6	36.4	34.2	32.2	27
Consumption	62.3	47.4	60.6	63.8	66.8	68.5
Consumption by residents	46.4	33.8	45.6	47.8	49.8	55
Government expenditure	15.9	13.6	15	16	17	18
Net exports	2.4	4.0	3.0	2	1	0

Sources: Data for 2000–2010 was sourced from the State Statistical Bureau, "China Statistical Abstract 2011", Beijing, China Statistics Press, 2011; 2015–2030 data are the estimates of the author

By then, it is likely that GDP calculated using the exchange rate method will exceed GDP calculated using the PPP current price or PPP constant price methods (1990 international dollar rates). This increase is faster and higher than actual GDP calculated using the constant price or constant exchange rate methods; it was hard to imagine 10 years (2000) ago that such gaps could have been narrowed so quickly.[9]

Largest Consumer Market in the World

At the heart of China's 12th Five-year Development Program is the concept of "expanding domestic demand. (Liu He 2011a)". This represents China's aim to shift from a "world factory" to a "world market" and from "Chinese exports" to "Chinese imports." This is good news for the world and a significant opportunity for China's development.

In the next 20 years, in terms of the expenditure components of GDP, China will move even further from an export-oriented economy toward a domestic demand-driven economy, and from an investment-driven economy[10] to a consumption-driven economy. It is expected that China's consumption rate will rise from 47.4% in 2010 to 63.8% by 2020, and to more than 70% by 2030. Consumption will rise from 33.8% in 2020 to 47.8% by 2030 and up to 55% by 2030. Government spending will rise from 13.6% in 2010 to 16% by 2020, and to 18% by 2030. Correspondingly, investment will drop from its current rate of 48.6 to 27%. China will enjoy a long-term trade balance, with net exports in GDP lower than 1% (Table 4.3).

---

[9] Many research organizations have underestimated China's economic aggregate. For instance, in 2008, the IMF said in its "Global Economic Outlook (2009)", that China will become the second largest economy in the world, and move into first place by 2050. However, China's GDP aggregate, calculated using the real exchange rate method, has already exceeded that of Japan to become the world's second largest economy.

[10] Since the beginning of the new century, with a new round of heavy industry and chemical industrialization, China's consumption rate has dropped from 62.3% in 2000 to 47.4% in 2010, while investments have increased from 35.3% in 2000 to 48.6% in 2010, exceeding consumption.

By 2020, China will replace the United States as the largest consumer market in the world, thus realizing the goal set by the 17th National Party Congress that, "the domestic market will rank in the front ranks in the world in terms of total size" (Hu Jingao 2007). If calculated using the exchange rate current price method,[11] China's consumption levels for 2010 were US$2.7 trillion. This will be US$7 trillion by 2015, making China the second largest consumer market in the world, second only to the United States.[12] By 2020, it will be US$14.5 trillion. By 2025, China will overtake the United States to become the biggest consumer market in the world (1.15 times that of the United States). If calculated using PPP of the World Bank standard, China's consumption will be double that of the United States by 2020. If calculated using the Maddison method, China's consumption will be 1.29 times that of the United States. If calculated using the above three methods, China's consumption will between 1.75 and 1.89 times greater than that of the United States by 2030 (Table 4.4).

The next 20 years will herald a golden age of consumption for China, with an increase in and the improvement of China's consumption structure.[13] The golden age will be supported by four major pillars: the increased income[14] and real consumption power of residents; an accelerated upgrade of the consumption structure to effect a true era of consumption;[15] an upward trend of marginal consumption; and a mutual reinforcement of private consumption and public consumption.

By using the unique advantages of being a world power brought about by domestic demand, China will become the No. 1 market in the world. By 2030, China's urban population will reach one billion, more than twice that of the United States, and greater than the total population of the 27 EU countries combined (501 million in 2010).

China will become the No. 1 importer in the world. Between 2006 and 2010, China's trade imports equaled US$5.78 trillion (US$1.39 trillion for 2010, accounting for 9.1% of the world's total, and already the second largest importer).[16] China's

---

[11] This method takes into account the changes in China's GDP deflator, and the change in the exchange rate between the RMB and US$ is the annual dollar price.

[12] According to an analysis by the Swiss Bank, by 2015 China's domestic consumption market will increase from 5.4% to approximately 15.6% to become the second largest consumer market in the world following the United States (Liu He 2011b).

[13] The average consumption of low-income countries is 75%; that of middle income countries is 66%, the investment of upper-middle income countries averages 22%, and is 80% for high-income countries (Jin Sanlin 2009).

[14] The 12th Five-year Development Program demands the synchronized growth of residents income and GDP.

[15] Since the beginning of the 21st century, China has been experiencing the upgrading of its consumption structure (dominated by the automotive, housing, and telecommunication sectors), with a consumption level of 10,000 yuan in the automotive, housing, and investment sectors (areas with the greatest levels of consumption). With a transition to higher incomes, residents' consumption will experience a further upgrade (number four), and a greater bias toward service consumption. Education, medical care, health, sports, culture, entertainment, and environmental protection will all experience greater consumption demand.

[16] US total imports in 2010 were US$196.81 billion, 12.6% of the world's total, 1.41 times that of China (State State Statistical Bureau 2011).

Table 4.4 Domestic consumption (US$) of China and the United States and the catch up coefficient relative to the United States (2000–2030)

		2000	2010	2015	2020	2025	2030
Domestic consumption (US$ trillion)							
Exchange rate method	China	0.7	2.7	7.0	14.5	25.9	48.5
(current price)	USA	8.4	12.5	15.2	18.6	22.6	27.7
PPP (current price)	China	1.9	4.6	9.5	15.8	23.8	37.7
(World Bank)	USA	8.4	12.3	14.0	15.7	17.9	20.2
PPP (1990 price)	China	2.7	5.1	9.1	13.5	18.0	25.1
(Maddison)	USA	6.8	8.1	9.1	10.4	11.7	13.3
Catch up co-efficient (USA = 100)							
Exchange rate method		8.9	22.0	45.7	77.7	114.5	175.2
(current price)							
PPP (current price)		22.2	37.6	67.7	100.1	133.4	186.7
(World Bank)							
PPP (1990 price)		39.3	62.7	99.8	129.6	153.0	189.1
(Maddison)							

Note: Data for the US was sourced from the World Bank, World Development Bank, 2011; 2010–2030 data for the USA are those for 1985–2007, averaged by 85.11%

import value for 2011–2015 will double again to reach US$10 trillion, and by 2012 or 2013, China will overtake the United States to become the world's No. 1. With its rapidly increasing imports, China will make an increasingly greater contribution to the global market. It will play a significant role in the global market and will create massive market demands and employment opportunities.[17] This is an important condition for the promotion of worldwide prosperity.

Largest Modern Industrial System in the World

China's economy will shift from industry to services, especially modern services. By 2030, industry will account for 5%, secondary industry for 33%, and tertiary industry for 62%. Thus, it may only take China approximately 80 years to complete its process of industrial modernization (whereas Western countries took more than 200 years). China's process has entailed the following stages: a great agricultural country (1949); a great industrial country (1978); a great industrial power (2010); and will progress to a further stage, that of a great country with modern services by 2030. In the near future, China will become a world power with modern services (2050).

---

[17] Since China joined WTO in 2001, China's annual average imports has been US$687 billion, creating 14 million jobs for related countries and regions (Jia 2010).

Table 4.5 China's primary, secondary and tertiary industries (2010–2030)

Unit: %					
	2010	2015	2020	2025	2030
Primary	10.2	8.31	6.98	5.93	5.05
Secondary	46.9	44.83	41.47	37.37	32.58
Tertiary	43.0	46.86	51.55	56.7	62.37

Note: Data for 2010 was sourced from the State Statistical Bureau, "China Statistical Abstract 2011", p. 22, Beijing, China Statistical Press, 2001; data for 2015–2030 are the estimates of the author

Table 4.6 China's employment structure (2009–2030)

Unit: %					
	2009	2015	2020	2025	2030
Primary	38.1	32.1	27.0	21.8	16.6
Secondary	27.8	29.0	29.9	30.8	31.6
Tertiary	34.1	38.9	43.1	47.4	51.8

Note: Data for 2010 was sourced from the State Statistical Bureau, "China Statistical Abstract 2011", p. 43, Beijing, China Statistical Press, 2001; data for 2015–2030 are the estimates of the author

Between 2011 and 2030, China's industrial structure will continue to improve, with a steady increase in tertiary industries.[18] By 2015, the proportion of tertiary industry will exceed that of secondary industry to become a leading industry. By 2030, tertiary industry will be the dominant player, representing 62.4% of industry. Correspondingly, the proportion of the primary industry will drop sharply, down to 8.8% by 2015 and 5.05% by 2030, similar to that of developed countries. Secondary industries will be relatively stable, with a slight decrease but still occupy a significant proportion of industry as a whole; it will drop from 44.83% in 2015 to 32.58% by 2030 (Table 4.5).

China's employment structure will be adjusted accordingly in 2011–2030.[19] Employment within the tertiary industry will exceed that of the primary industry by 2012 and employment within the secondary industry will exceed that of the primary industry by 2018. An upgrade of the industrial structure will demand a decrease in employment rates within the primary industry, from 32.1% in 2015 to 16.6% by 2030. Employment in the secondary and tertiary industries will further rise, especially within the tertiary industry, from 29.0 and 38.9% in 2015 to 31.6% and 51.8% by 2030, respectively (Table 4.6).

[18] At present, China is still behind in terms of the development of its tertiary industry, with plenty of room for improvement. In 2010, tertiary industry was responsible for 4.3.0% of China's GDP while that of middle income countries was 50%, and high-income countries reached 70% (see Mao Jiantang 2011).

[19] At present, the employment rates in the secondary and tertiary industries are on the low side. In 2009, employment within the three industries (primary, secondary, and tertiary) was 38.1%, 27.8%, and 34.1%, respectively. The employment rate proportion of the primary industry is too high and that of secondary industries is at the 1870–1910 levels of the United States. The employment rate proportion of the tertiary industry is far lower than in developed countries (which is between 60 and 80%).

Table 4.7 International comparison of added value shares of knowledge-intensive and high technology-intensive industries (1995–2030)

Unit: %						
Country	1995	2000	2007	2010	2020	2030
China	19.9	21.7	23.3	25	30	35
USA	34	36.6	38.4	39	41	42
EU	26.9	28.8	29.7	30	33	36
Japan	25.5	28.1	28.2	29	32	34

Note: (1) EU includes 27 countries; (2) definition of knowledge-intensive and high-tech intensive industries follows that of the OECD (Organization for Economic Co-operation and Development)

Sources: Data for 1995–2007 was sourced from IHS Global Insight, World Industry Service database National Science Foundation (NSF), Science and Engineering Indicators 2010; data for 2010–2030 are the estimates of the author

China will further develop seven strategic industries. These industries currently represent 4% of GDP (2010), but this will increase to 8% by 2015, and should further increase to approximately 15%. Thus, the four pillar industries (energy efficiency and environmental protection, a new generation of information technology, biological, and high-end manufacturing industries) will become more concrete and three new prominent industries (new energy sources, new materials and new energy vehicles) will be created. With these core industries, China's industrial structure will become a knowledge-intensive, resource-intensive and ecologically-friendly industrial system that will satisfy the demands of sustainable development.

China also intends to stimulate its technology industry to move from equipment and manufacturing toward independent R&D, integration, and innovations to increase the share of the technology industry's added value in GDP. A knowledge economy is essential to advance knowledge-intensive industries and to stimulate the reform of industrial and employment structures. The proportion of knowledge-intensive industries should be increased. The shares of China's high-tech industry and knowledge-intensive industry in GDP rose from 19.9% in 1995 to 23.3% in 2007. We estimate that it may have reached 25% in 2010 and will increase to 30 and 35% by 2020 and 2030, respectively (Table 4.7). By then, the added value shares of knowledge-intensive and high technology industries in GDP will reach the levels of EU countries and Japan, and the gap with the United States will reduce by at least 7 percentage points. This marks a shift from material factor input (resources, labor and capital) to knowledge and innovation inputs.

China will seek to accelerate the development of its green industries. While China has already established some foundations for such development, it represents a new beginning in China's development process, and there is huge potential.[20] It is necessary to develop green industries, characterized with low resource consumption, less pollution, and better economic efficiency. In addition, such development will

---

[20] It is estimated that in the next 5 years, China's energy-efficient and environmental protection industries will have a total value of 4 trillion yuan (see Li Keqiang 2010).

Table 4.8 Number of world's top 500 per country (1975–2011)

	1975	1980	1990	2000	2005	2011
USA	241	217	164	179	177	133
Japan	54	66	111	108	81	68
UK	49	51	43	38	35	31
Germany	38	38	30	37	36	34
France	29	29	30	37	39	35
Canada	17	20	12	12	13	11
China		1	1	11	21	69
Mainland				10	18	57
HK						4
Taiwan		1	1	1	3	8
South Korea		6	11	11	11	14
India	2	2	6	1	5	8

Source: data were sourced from the Forbes databank, see Fortune, Fortune Global 500 Database, http://www.timeinc.net/fortune/datastore/ds/global.html

also cultivate some new areas of economic growth. Strict measures should be adopted to restrict the development of energy-sapping industries (iron and steel, building materials, non-metallic mines, chemical and petro-chemical)[21]; its pace should be accelerated to ensure that China does not become locked in energy-intensive, carbon emission-intensive and capital-intensive models.

At the core of a country's ascent lies the rise of exceptional and well-known enterprises, especially world-class enterprises. An important hallmark for a country is an increase in the number of enterprises entering the world's top 500 companies. Conversely, a country's decline parallels a decline in the number of enterprises among the world's top 500 (Table 4.8).

China will become the country with the largest number of enterprises among the world's top 500 companies. In 1995, China had four companies in the top 500, including two on the mainland. By 2011, there were 69, overtaking Japan to rank second in the world. Of these, 57 are on the mainland, including those administered by the central government and a number of local state-owned and private enterprises.[22] Four are in Hong Kong and eight in Taiwan. They receive investments from and are managed on the Chinese mainland, and are very successful. In the future, the state will adopt key measures to support a number of internationally competitive

---

[21] Energy-sapping industries refers to energy consumption within total industrial consumption, which is 1.5 times the proportion of industrial output in total industrial output. For instance, China's iron and steel industry, building materials, and non-metallic mines, and chemical and petrochemical industries in 2005 accounted for only 20% of the total industrial added value, but its energy consumption accounted for 33% of the total energy consumption (IEA 2007).

[22] Local state-owned enterprises include Shanghai Auto Industry Group, Hebei Iron and Steel group, Henan Coal and Coal Chemicals Group Co. Ltd., Jizhong Energy Group, and Zhejiang Real Estate Group; private enterprises including Huawei Group, Shagang Group, and Lenovo Group.

Table 4.9 Urban population of China and the United States (1950–2030)

Year	Urban population (millions)			Urbanization rate (%)		% of world urban population	
	China	USA	China/USA (time)	China	USA	China	USA
1950	61.7	101.2	0.61	11.2	64.2	8.37	13.74
1960	130.7	130.3	1.00	19.7	70.0	13.12	13.08
1970	144.2	154.6	0.93	17.4	73.6	10.83	11.61
1980	191.4	170.3	1.12	19.4	73.7	11.00	9.78
1990	302.0	192.8	1.57	26.4	75.3	13.28	8.48
2000	459.1	225.3	2.04	36.2	79.1	16.09	7.90
2010	665.6	259.0	2.57	49.7	82.3	19.05	7.41
2020	845.0	290.7	2.91	60.0	84.9	21.00	6.91
2030	1020.0	318.5	3.20	70.0	87.0	22.90	6.41

Data sources: data for the USA and the total world population are based on UN Department of Economic and Social Affairs, "World Urbanization Prospects: The 2008 Revision"; 1950–2010 data for China were sourced from the State Statistical Bureau: "Collected Statistical Data of the 60 Years of News China", Beijing, China Statistical Press, 2009; State Statistical Bureau, "6th National Population Census Bulletin", April 28, 2011; data for 2020–2030 are the estimates of the author, of which data for the growth rate for 2010–2030 will be 2.15 % and 4.35 % for 1978–2010

enterprises with their own intellectual property rights and famous brands, and assist them to become listed among the world's top 500 and 2,000 companies.[23] Our most conservative estimate is that by 2020, China will have more than 120 mainland enterprises included in the world's top 500. Accompanied by those companies in Hong Kong and Taiwan, the number of Chinese top 500 enterprises will exceed that of the United States, to rank first in the world. By 2030, China's entries in the top 500 enterprises will exceed that of the United States during its peak, equivalent to China's world total shares regarding economic aggregate, trade, and investment.

Largest Urban Population in the World

In terms of urban population, China surpassed the United States in 1974 to become the world No. 1. By 2010, China's urban population had reached 670 million, 19.5% of the total worldwide urban population or twice that of the United States. By 2030, China's urban population will reach more than 900 million, representing 22.9% of the world's population, three times that of the United States, and four times the total urban population of the United States. In addition, the gap between the urbanization rates of the United States and China have been narrowed: 53.0% in 1950, 54.35% in 1980, and 32.6% in 2010. By 2030, China's urbanization rate will reach 70%, with the gap with the United States narrowed to 17.0% (Table 4.9).

---

[23] The World's Top 2000 is published by the American "Forbes" magazine, including the largest and strongest listed companies in the world in terms of sales revenue, profits, assets, and market value.

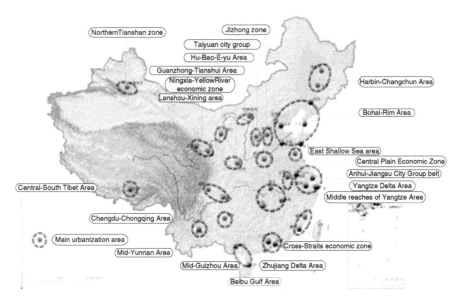

Fig. 4.1 "Two-horizontal and three-vertical axes" urbanization strategic pattern (Source: Outlined 12th five-year program of economic and social development)

China is still in an acceleration period in terms of city groupings. This is quite different from the urbanization strategy used for building small towns put forward 10 years ago. It is also different from the traditional urban strategy or urbanization strategy. Modern factors converge within city groups and economic zones (an economic zone can be reached within 1 h by express highway, high-speed rail, and other means of transportation). This includes huge city groups with a population of at least 80 million, such as city groups in the Zhujiang (Pearl) River Delta, the Yangtze River Delta, and Bohai Rim, which will become the flagships of social and economic development, and important sources of innovation. Additionally, these areas are characterized by high population and economic concentrations, and economic zones; these factors have a significant influence on China and worldwide (Zhang Ping 2011, p. 197). There are four levels of city groups: super-large city groups, each with a population of 50–70 million, extra-large city groups each with a population of 20–40 million, large city groups each with a population of eight million, and intermediate city groups each with a population of one million.[24] From a long-term point of view, the GDP of large city groups will represent more than 80% of the national total by 2020, their trade and financial revenue will both represent more than 90 %. By 2030, these percentages will have increased again.

In terms of functional zones, there will be a two-horizontal and three-vertical city-group pattern (Fig. 4.1). Two horizontal city groups refer to cities along the two

---

[24] In 2008, the number of cities with only urban populations in the city proper reached 122, 18.6 % of China's 655 cities.

horizontal axes: Eurasian Continental Bridge and the Yangtze River; the three vertical axes are coasts (from Dalian to Zhanjiang), Beijing-Harbin, Beijing-Guangzhou, and Hohhot-Baotou-Kunming. There will be state-priority development areas and key development areas. The reshaping of the economic geography of the New China, dominated by city groups, is perhaps the most significant economic geographical change to involve the world's largest population, the largest number of major cities, sea, land, and air transportation systems, urban/rural integration, and regional integration and international integration. This process will become a powerful force behind China's sustainable development.

World's Largest and Most Modern Infrastructure

China already possesses the world's largest modern infrastructure, which is connected to the production, distribution, exchange, and consumption of the national economy, promoting the largest-scaled spatial movement of people, materials, and information in a highly efficient manner. This infrastructure has stimulated China's economic and social development, and has ensured and improved the livelihood of the people. In addition, it has a special role in national defense.

In 2008, American New York Times columnist Thomas L. Friedman wrote, "Just compare arriving at La Guardia's dumpy terminal in New York City and driving through the crumbling infrastructure into Manhattan with arriving at Shanghai's sleek airport and taking the 220-mile-per-hour magnetic levitation train, which uses electromagnetic propulsion instead of steel wheels and tracks, to get to town in a blink. Then ask yourself: Who is living in the third world country? (Friedman 2008)"

In 2008, China's infrastructure could have been described as, "the rich parts of China, the modern parts of Beijing or Shanghai or Dalian, are now more state-of-the art than rich America" (Friedman 2008). However, in another 20 years or so, it will be "a matter of course for China to catch up from behind" (Zhou Enlai 1998) and with less sunk costs, more advanced technologies, and a greater ability to build the world's biggest and most modern infrastructure, China will possess a system that will overshadow that of the United States in every way.

By 2030, with the exception of its railways, China's main communications, energy, and information infrastructures will rank first in the world, with the largest and the most modern integrated communications and telecommunications system, that will sport faultless networks, and be well structured and interconnected.

China will also 1 day possess the world's largest and the most modern state high-speed railway network. China has already become a leader in the building of high-speed railways. At present, the operational mileage of high-speed railways is 6,920 km, ranking first in the world. By 2012, the operational mileage of passenger trains and inter-city railways (at a speed of 200 km/hr) will reach 13,000 km (and 20,000 km by 2020). By 2030, a rapid railway network will link all the major cities and service the majority of the population.

Table 4.10 Operational
mileage of China's railways
and highways (1978–2030)

Unit: 10,000 km				
Year	Railway	Fast railway	Highway	Express highway
1978	5.17		89.02	
1990	5.78		102.83	0.05
2000	6.87			1.63
2005	7.54		334	4.10
2010	9.12		401	7.41
2015	12	4.5		8.3
2020	13	6.0	450	8.5
2030	15	7.5	500	10

Sources: State Statistical Bureau: China Statistical Abstract 2010; Ministry of Communications and Transport (2010), Ministry of Railways (2010); 2015 data were sourced from the 12th Five-year Development Program; data for 2020 and 2030 are the estimates of the author

In 2009, China's express highway measured only 7,000 km. However, by 2015, it will reach 45,000 km, forming a state express railway network that will link up all provincial capitals, basically servicing all cities with a population of more than 500,000 (Zhang Ping 2011, p. 136). With the rapid development of urbanization and the expansion of city groups, the system will effectively stimulate communication networks among cities and the main cities in city groups. Further, it will encourage communication among large- and medium-sized cities and smaller cities and towns. By 2030, China's express highway will measure 75,000 km (Table 4.10).

China will soon have the world's largest and the most modern high-speed highway networks. In 2007, the United States had 75,000 km of express highways (CIA 2009). As of 2010, China's express highways had an operational mileage of 74,000 km, more than a quarter of the world's total express highways (200,000 km). By 2015, China will have built a high-speed highway network exceeding 80,000 km, linking up provincial capital cities, covering all cities with populations greater than 200,000. By 2030, the total mileage will exceed 100,000 km (Table 4.10).

China's highway network is already the longest "green highway" network in the world. In 2008, 1.68 million km of roads were covered with green, 45.0% of the total road mileage.[25] China has put forward a strategic concept for its main functional zones, which aims to have most roads covered with green by 2030. In addition, the express highways that are to be jointly built by China and its neighboring countries will effectively stimulate the building of express highway networks in Asia.

China has already become the world No. 1 in terms of the freight and container throughput capacities of its ports. The throughput capacities of China's ports of designated size increased from 483.21 million tons in 1990 to 4754.81 million tons

---

[25] Ministry of Communications and Transport, "Statistical Bulletin of 2008 Highway and Waterway Transport Development", February 29, 2009.

in 2009. As of 2009, 15 coastal ports each had a throughput capacity of 100 million tons compared with only three in 2000 (State Statistical Bureau 2010).

Other modern infrastructure networks will also be expanded. They include petroleum pipelines, oil product pipelines, and natural gas pipelines. Airports, and domestic and foreign airlines, will boost passenger numbers and cargo transport. A three-in-one national information network with super broadband at its core will begin to take shape. By 2020, China's total power installation capacity will reach 1.6 billion kW to become the world's No. 1. The state power grid will invest RMB 4 trillion in the next 10 years in smart-power grids to make the biggest unified smart grid in the world.[26] The smart grid (with ultra-high voltage at its core) and the on-going intensive development and construction of large-scale hydropower, nuclear power, and wind power projects will create trans-regional ultra-high voltage transmission channels.[27] By 2015, China will complete the construction of 200,000 km of 330 kW and above power transmission lines to become the world's largest ultra-high power transmission network. By 2030, China will have extended the 330 kW transmission lines to 400,000 km. In addition, China and its neighboring countries will complete a number of international power transmission lines and energy transport channels.

In a word, the next 20 years will remain the golden age for the construction of China's infrastructure. It will become an important source of domestic demand, and will effectively stimulate the development of all production factors, creating favorable conditions with which to form a national unified market. China will see balanced development between cities and countryside, and among different regions, thus reshaping China's economic geography. The rejuvenation of China's infrastructure will become the corner stone of China's modernization.

Summary: Toward a World Economic Power

Over the next 20 years, China will maintain its high growth, with average annual rates between 7 and 8% (2011–2020 at approximately 8.0% and 2020–2030 at approximately 7.0%). If calculated using the constant price method, by 2030 China's GDP will be more than four times the base figure of 2010. If 1978 is used as the base figure, the China's 2030 GDP will be more than 80 times the base figure. Thus, it would be true to say that there will be no other country capable of increasing its

---

[26] The smart grid has become a new development trend, featuring information, automation, interaction, and networks that are highly efficient, economical, clean, and safe.

[27] For example, southwest China integrated energy will be transmitted to east China, central China, and Guangdong Province; the Erdos Basin, Shanxi, and the eastern Inner Mongolia integrated energy bases will transmit power to north China, east China and central China; the Xinjiang integrated energy base will transmit power to central China (see Zhang Ping 2011, p. 128).

economic aggregate by more than 80 times in a mere 52 years. This is double the 40 times growth co-efficient of the GDP growth for the 12 Western European countries in the 172 years from 1820 to 1992 (Angus Maddison 1995).

By 2030, China will be a strong modern economic power in the real sense of the term. By taking into account the changes in the GDP growth rate and GDP deflator, exchange rate changes between RMB and US$, and by calculating the constant RMB price and constant dollar price using the previously mentioned three methods (exchange rate at current US dollar price, PPP at current dollar price, and PPP constant dollar price), we predict that before 2020, China will overtake the United States in terms of GDP aggregate (between 1 and 17 times greater). Thus, China will end the United States' 100-year dominance. By 2030, China's GDP aggregate will be approximately 2.0–2.2 times that of the United States.

In addition, China will become the largest consumer market, and the world's largest modern industrial system. It will have the greatest number of enterprises listed in the world's top 500 companies. It will be home to the largest-scaled urbanization. China will build the world's largest and most modern infrastructure.

China is heading toward a golden age of development in which new forms of industrialization, urbanization, knowledge and information, global economic integration, and infrastructure modernization will continue to flourish and grow. China's widespread development will have good momentum, and be well coordinated, innovative, and green. It will be dedicated to political civilization, social harmony, a flourishing culture, and ecological security.

References

Angang Hu (2001) Future China economic growth determined by TFP. China Natl Stud (46), May 30
Angang Hu, Wu Yilong (2010) China: toward 2015, chapter IV. In: Background for 12th five-year plan period. Zhejiang People's Publishing House, Hangzhou, pp 68–104
China State Statistical Bureau (2011) China statistical abstract 2011. China Statistics Press, Beijing, p 24
CIA (2009) The world factbook. CIA, Washington, DC
Deng Xiaoping (1986) One country, two systems, June 22–23, 1984. In: Selected documents since the 12th national party congress. People's Publishing House, Beijing, pp 512–615
Friedman TL (2008) A biblical seven years. New York Times, Aug
Hu Jingao (2007) Hold high the great banner of socialism with Chinese characteristics and strive to win new victories in building a complete well-off society. Report to the 17th national congress of the Chinese community party, Oct 15
Japanese Society for the Study of National Conditions (2011) Japan's 100 years. Tokyo, p 264 May 17
Jia Qinglin (2010) Persisting in peaceful development to realize win-win. Speech at the opening ceremony of the 21st Century Forum, 7 Sept, 2010
Jin Sanlin (2009) Changing characteristics and development trend of China's investment and consumption. Dev Stud (10)
Li Keqiang (2010) Problems concerning restructuring to stimulate sustainable development. Qiu Shi
Liu He (2011) Raising the percentage of middle-income people and expanding domestic market – basic logic of the 12th five-year development program (proposed). China 50 Econ Forum (86), 11 Apr

Liu He (2011) Raising the income of the middle-income people and expanding the domestic market – the basic logic of the 12th five-year development program (proposed). China 50 Econ Forum (86), 11 Apr

Ma Jiantang (2011a) Get a comprehensive understanding of China's status in the world economy. People's Daily, 17 Mar

Maddison A (1995) Monitoring the world economy 1820–1992. OECD Development Centre, Paris

Mao Jiantang (2011b) A full understanding of China's position in the world economy. People's Daily, 17 Mar

Mao Zedong (1977) Strengthen party unity, carry forward party traditions, August 30, 1956. In: Selected works of Mao Zedong, vol 5, 1st edn. Foreign Languages Press, Beijing, pp 314–315

Spence M (2008) China's successful experience in reform and opening up and its new challenges. In: 50 people review China's 30 years of development: review and analysis. China Economic Press, China, p 45

State Statistical Bureau (2010) China statistical abstract 2011. China Statistics Press, Beijing, p 24

State Statistical Bureau (2011) China statistical abstract 2011. China Statistics Press, Beijing, p 24

Wang Xiaolu, Fan Gang, Liu Peng (2009) Shift of China's growth model and growth sustainability. Econ Stud (1):4–16

Zhang Ping (ed) (2011) Reader guide to the Outlined 12th five-year development program for economic and social development of the People's Republic of China. People's Publishing House, Beijing

Zhou Enlai (1998) Government work report December 21–22, 1964. In: CPC central documentation office selected important documents since the founding of New China, vol 19. Central Documentation Press, p 491

Chapter 5
The World's Strongest Innovative Power

It is a matter of course for late comers to catch up. Our country has many superior conditions and we should be more confident of catching up and overtaking science and technically advanced countries in a not too long a time. Simply put, we must use score of years to catch up with and overtake the levels that took Western bourgeoisie several hundred years to attain (Mao Zedong 1996).

Mao Zedong (1964)

Innovation must become the main driving force behind economic and social development and knowledge innovation must become the core factor for building up the country competitive power.

Hu Jintao (2011)

International competition has become fiercer with the onset of the twenty-first century. The essence of this competition lies in the area of science and technology. Whoever scales the peak of global science and technology innovation will become the leader in global economic development. China is now becoming a forerunner in such areas. In 2006, the Chinese government published the "Outlined Medium- and Long-Term Program for Scientific and Technological Development (2006–2020)", drawing a grand blueprint for building an innovative country. The United States,[1]

---

[1] In September 2009, the US government published "A Strategy for American Innovation: Driving Towards Sustainable Growth and Quality Jobs", promising to "educate the next generation with twenty-first century knowledge and skills while creating a world-class workforce" and to "invest three **percent of GDP in R&D."**

A. Hu et al., *China 2030*, DOI 10.1007/978-3-642-31328-8_5,

Japan[2] and the EU[3] have since followed with similar directive documents regarding developments in science and technology.

Thomson Reuters released a report "Patented in China" in 2010, which stated that,

> Clearly, an epic industrial revolution has brought China to its current state of development, but it will be China's intellectual revolution that will carry it forward (Eve Zhou and Bob Stembridge 2010).

China, as an innovator, is creating a comprehensive and multi-dimensional development scheme that will make full use of China's unique institutional advantages. In 2010, after formulating and implementing its science and technology development plans, the Chinese government went on to promulgate and implement the "State Medium- and Long-term Human Resources Development Program (2010–2020)" (June 2010) and the "State Medium- and Long-term Educational Reform and Development Program (2010–2020)" (July 2010). Together with the State Medium- and Long-Term Science and Technology Development Program (2006–2020), China has clearly set itself three major goals to create a powerhouse in terms of human resources, knowledgeable and skilled people, and innovative science and technology projects. Thus, China has established a policy system featuring mutual reliance and mutual reinforcement in education, personnel, and science and technology. The three major development programs constitute integrated innovation, fully embodying three core ideas as follows: "science and technology are the key; education is the foundation and personnel are fundamental."[4] These three concepts demonstrate the top-level design and system planning involved in the national development strategy; each has its own goal and emphasis, but they are interconnected. While they are mutually supportive and echo each other, the three concepts have their own characteristics. They will provide strong guidance to China on its course to become a world innovative power.

---

[2] In February 2010, the Japanese government published the "Fourth Basic Outlined Program for Science and Technology Development", stating to further intensify investments and the training of special talents.

[3] In March 2010, the EU Commission published "Strategic Plan 2020", which listed a series of objectives regarding research and innovation and funding and employment. In addition, it stated that R&D expenditure should increase from 1.9% of GDP to 3%, and that the percentage of those with just a basic education should not exceed 10%, and at least 40% of the people aged 30–34 years should receive a higher education.

[4] Premier Wen Jiabao said at the National Personnel Work Conference that in the present-day world international competition is becoming fiercer each day; this level of competition can be seen in science and technology, education, and personnel. Science and technology holds the key; education serves as the foundation and personnel are fundamental. The State Medium- and Long-term Personnel Development Program and the State Medium- and Long-term Science and Technology Development Program have already been issued and implemented, and along with the State Medium- and Long-term Education Reform and Development Program, mutually support each other and are closely related, with each having its own emphasis. They represent top-level design and system planning in state development. People's Net, May 27, 2010.

Over the next 20 years, human resources, personnel, and innovation in science and technology will become key factors to help China realize its significant development objectives, and achieve great prosperity and shared wealth. By 2020, China will have become a country characterized by its pioneering science and technology projects. By 2030, China will have become a strong innovative world power; China's human resources aggregate, the aggregate of competent personnel, and the strength of its science and technology, will represent one-third of the world's total, (which, similar to its GDP percentage of the world's total GDP, will be greater than its share of the world's population percentage).

A World Leader in Human Resources

After 2020, China's population dividend effect will begin to fade. China is the most populated country in the world, and with this comes "population dividends," the main factor behind its economic takeoff.[5] However, the rapid growth in population has determined that China's "population dividend period" will come early and will last for a shorter time. As a result, a period of population burden will also arrive early. China has been experiencing a population dividend peak since 2000. The proportion of working age population in the total population will reach its peak between 2010 and 2015. It will then decline, and after 2020 the population dividend effect will gradually fade, with a steady decline in the working age population. By 2030, the proportion of the working age population in the total population will drop from its peak of 74.5 to 67.2%, and will continue to drop to 61.4% by 2050.

In addition, China will enter a period of population aging and lower birth rates, which will become a great challenge. The proportion of the population aged 65 years and above will rise from 8.9% in 2010 to 15.9% by 2030; the proportion of children aged 14 years and under will rise from 16.6% in 2010 to 19.0% by 2015, before dropping steadily to 18.7% by 2020 and 16.9% by 2030 (Table 5.1).

> The years of education received by the population, especially working age population, reflect the aggregate and the capacity of absorbing and applying advanced technologies of the skilled laborers. (Barro and Jong-Wha Lee 2010)

While the population dividend effect is gradually fading, the rapid development of education, competent personnel, and science and technology will bring about dividends in the preferred form of newly added values, that is, human capital dividends. Human capital dividends include education dividends (a greater share of the population has attained higher levels of education), and employment dividends (the percentage of employed population in the total population). The higher the human

---

[5] In a general sense, the population dividend period is based on the proportion of the working age population in the total population. It drops with a drop in the birth rate. When the working age population (15–64 years) reaches 60%, it is considered to enter a period of population dividend.

Table 5.1 China's population structure and world total percentages (2010–2030)

Unit: %

Year	Total population in world's total	Working age population in world's total	Children's population (0–14 years) in world's total	Working age population (15–64 years) in world's total	Aged population (65 years and over) in world's total
2010	19.6	21.5	16.6	74.5	8.9
2015	19.1	20.8	19.0	71.5	9.4
2020	18.6	19.8	18.7	69.6	11.7
2025	18.1	18.9	18.1	68.6	13.4
2030	17.6	18.0	16.9	67.2	15.9

Sources: UN, World Population Prospects: The 2008 Revision Population Database; 2010 data for China were sourced from the Main Data Bulletin of the 6th National Population Census (No. 1), April 28, 2011

Table 5.2 Total human capital of China, USA and EU in the world's total (1950–2030)

Unit: %

	1950	1980	1990	2000	2010	2020	2030
China	6.0	17.6	20.0	24.1	24.1	26.8	27.2
USA	22.7	16.9	14.1	11.5	9.3	8.1	7.0
EU	32.4	20.2	17.4	15.3	13.7	12.4	11.8
China/USA	0.27	1.04	1.42	2.10	2.58	3.31	3.89

Note: (1) total human capital of working age population = education attainment of population aged 15 years and above × population aged 25 and above; (2) EU includes 27 countries
Sources: Barro and Jong-Wha Lee (2010); UN, World Population Prospects: The 2008 Revision Population Database; data for 2020 and 2030 are the estimates of the author

capital stock, the higher the added value of labor productivity and labor output, and the higher the economic output created by each unit of labor. Thus, the higher the employed population, the stronger the vitality of the economy. The human capital dividend is in fact a higher quality population dividend. The marginal efficiency of a human capital dividend is significantly higher than that of a population dividend.

China's percentage of human capital stock in the world's total has been increasing, generating a new education dividend. Here, we define the human capital aggregate of a country as the average years of education received by the nationals multiplied by the working age population. This indicator not only reflects the amount of labor but also, to a certain extent, the quality of labor. In 2010, the education attainment of Chinese nationals reached 9 years. We estimate that it could reach 10 years by 2020 and up to 11 years by 2030. In 2010, the share of Chinese total human capital represented 24.1% of the world's total, 2.58 times that of the United States. It will reach 27.2% by 2030, 3.89 times that of the United States. Although the shares of total population and working age population in the world's total will steadily decline (Table 5.1), the share of China's human resources in the world total will assume an upward trend, because education dividends will play a crucial role (Table 5.2).

China's higher ratio of employed population will offset, to a certain extent, the negative effect of the aging population. Due to changes in the population structure, the ratio of China's working age population to non-working age population will reach its peak between 2010 and 2015 and will then rapidly decline. However, the ratio of employed population to non-employed population will be maintained at approximately 1.4 times for 40 years after it reached 1.3 times in 1990, without a significant drop. Between 2010 and 2030, the percentage of the employed population in the total population will remain relatively stable at 59% (see Fig. 5.1). With an increase in the mean life expectancy, average healthy life expectancy (see Chap. 6, Table 6.5), and average education attainment, the proportion of the population who retire later in life will also increase, thus maintaining the employment dividend for a longer period.

The share of urban and non-agricultural employment will also steadily increase, generating a new employment transfer dividend. China's working age population will begin to drop and total employment growth will remain relatively low. However,

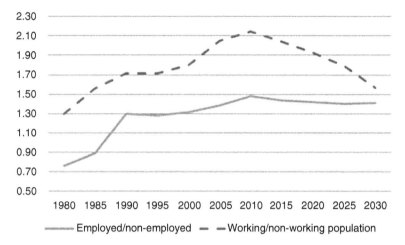

Fig. 5.1 Ratio of employed and unemployed population and the ratio of working age and non-working age population (Sources: UN, World Population Prospects: The 2008 Revision Population Database; State Statistical Bureau, "China Statistical Abstract 2011", p. 43, Beijing, China Statistical Press, 2011; data for 2015–2030 are the estimates of the author)

the number of rural employees and agricultural laborers is high (470 million and 300 million in 2009, respectively). The transfer of rural laborers to cities and towns, and agricultural laborers to non-agricultural activities, will create an employment transfer dividend (i.e., a transfer from low productivity to high labor productivity). This will increase labor productivity by 2–5 times, thus becoming an important source for the growth of total factor productivity.

A Strong Power in Knowledgeable and Skilled People

In the course of societal development, knowledgeable and skilled people are the driving force behind social progress, people's wealth and happiness, and the prosperity of a nation. The present-day world is entering a period of great development, great changes, and great adjustment. The multi-polarization of the world and economic globalization are moving deeper into their development; science and technology are advancing day-by-day; the knowledge economy is beginning to develop. Of all the national strategic resources, knowledgeable and skilled people are the most important (see Box 5.1). The acceleration of the development of knowledgeable and skilled people is a key strategy to gain an advantage in the fierce international competition.

A populous country is not necessarily a strong country. The population may become a heavy burden to a country's development. Only by increasing investment in human capital, via developments in education and training more personnel, is it possible for a nation to become truly strong. China's reform and opening up over the

Box 5.1 Definition of Ren Cai, a Primary Resource

We define ren cai as people with positive externalities, capable of creating added social values. The term has a triple meaning: first, those that generate positive externalities with a strong spillover effect, and in China they generate a significant nationwide effect; second, ren cai creates social values, including economic values, science values, cultural values, and ecological values, which are of social significance and not confined to an individual or a family; and third, the social values they create are newly added values, belonging to the concept of flow volume rather than the constant stock of the original value. Thus, the so-called outstanding ren cai are those who can create important and newly added social values, and generate greater externalities, and a scale effect.

Ren cai is closest to the term "professional" in Western languages, which refers to those who have received specialized education or training, with high skills in a certain area, but excluding agriculturally skilled workers or trades people. In China, ren cai has an innovative broader meaning. It includes specialists and skilled agricultural and technical workers who have received intermediate-level vocational education. This enlarges the ramifications of the term as it includes laborers who have received specialized training and/or have acquired certain skills, thus turning the comparative advantage of labor into competitive advantages in promoting economic development.

At present, the concept of *ren cai* is divided into six areas and two levels. The six areas include party, government and corporate management, specialized skills (including natural sciences, engineering and social sciences), rural and highly skilled, and social organizations. What merits special mentioning is that regarding social organization (also called non-governmental organizations or non-profit seeking organizations), the term *ren cai* does not only refer to management staff with governmental backgrounds but also to the leaders and managers of grassroots non-governmental or non-profit seeking organizations. Future *ren cai* development strategies must pay careful attention to the important roles of social organizations in social reconstruction and development, and incorporate these leaders and managers into the national *ren cai* development strategy. The two levels refer to high-performance staff and specialized staff, who are useful in certain areas. These people may assume complementary roles in China's social progress and development.

past 30 years show that China's population has grown both in terms of size and education attainment, with qualified personnel coming to the fore in all industries and services. The introduction of the labor market and competition mechanism has released the creative power of the people, thus creating a unique social environment for innovative personnel to showcase their talents.

China will soon have the largest number of researchers in the world. Although China has been a significant power in terms of S&T human resources,[6] it currently does not have enough scientists and engineers engaging in research and experimental development. It is the "short board" of the barrel of personnel. In 2007, the full-time equivalents of R&D personnel in China made up just 0.1% of the total population, while that of the United States and the EU were 0.5 and 0.3%, respectively. However, this situation will soon be reversed. The full-time equivalents of R&D personnel are steadily increasing, with the numbers for 2000 twice that of 1980, and these doubled again by 2007. This growth is the fastest among all major countries and regions. In 2008, China overtook the EU and the United States to become the country with the greatest number of full-time equivalents in R&D personnel.

By 2030, the number of people in China receiving tertiary education will reach 300 million, the number of specialized and technical personnel will reach 120 million, the full-time equivalents in research and experimental development will reach four million/year,[7] and the number of scientists and engineers will have reached 3.5 million/year. By then, China will boast the biggest contingent of innovative personnel. China's R&D personnel will represent 35% of the world's total by 2030, equal to the combined numbers of the United States, the EU, and Japan (Table 5.3).

China will transition from a central power in terms of human resources to a dominant power. The general goal for future human resources development is to cultivate a large contingent that is optimal in structure, rational in distribution, and superior in quality. China will establish a comparative advantage in personnel competition and rank among the top counties in terms of human resources, thus laying a foundation for the realization of socialist modernization by the middle of this century. This development will include the following four trends: a steady increase in the aggregates of qualified personnel or rapid growth, and the constant expansion of personnel numbers; significant improvements in the quality of personnel and furthering the optimization of the structure; an obvious enhancement of the comparative advantage in personnel competition; and significant improvements in the efficacy of personnel use.

It may take three steps to achieve such development. First, the objectives of the 12th Five-year Development Program need to be met; the second step is to realize the goal for 2020 set in the State Medium- and Long-term Human Resources

---

[6] The main indicators for science and technology human capital include head count of R&D personnel and full-time equivalents of R&D personnel. According to a study by UNESCO, to measure human capital in science and technology by head count of R&D personnel could result in an underestimation and to measure human capital in science and technology by full-time equivalents of R&D personnel could result in an overestimation.

[7] The full-time equivalents of R&D personnel are a main indictor to measure S&T input. It refers to the total number of full-time personnel in research and experimental development and non-full-time personnel converted by work volume. It is the oft-used indicator to compare S&T human resources input.

Table 5.3 World total percentages for full-time R&D scientists and engineers of the five major economies (1995–2030)

Unit: %

	1995	2000	2005	2007	2020	2030
China	10.2	10.1	13.5	19.7	30.0	35.0
USA	18.3	18.4	16.5	19.8	15.0	12.0
EU	19.6	15.8	15.7	20.1	15.0	15.0
Japan	18.4	15.2	12.3	14.6	10.0	8.0
Russia	10.5	7.3	5.6	6.5	5.0	5.0

Sources: (1) data for 1995 and 2000 are converted from researchers per million population sourced from the World Bank, World Development Indicator 2010; (2) data for 2007 was sourced from UNESCO, Science, Technology and Gender: An International Report; data for 2020 and 2030 are the estimates of the author

Development Program (2010–2020); and the third step is to bring the total number of human resources to 270 million by 2030, with its percentage of the total population reaching 18, and 35% of the total employment rate (that is, the percentage of highly skilled personnel in the skilled labor force to reach 35%). In addition, the number of R&D personnel per 10,000 laborers will reach 55/year, double that of 2008, and the percentage of mainly working age population receiving tertiary education will reach 30%. The investment in human capital will reach 18% of GDP and personnel contributions will represent 40% of GDP (Table 5.4).[8]

China already possesses the economic, social and political conditions, as well as the rare (stable) international environment, to become a leading power in terms of qualified personnel. First, China has already established a socialist economic market, which contains a significant unified personnel market, one that is fair, fluid, and competitive. This market is capable of providing the overwhelming majority of people with an unprecedented stage on which to display their talents. Second, China's education system will develop both rapidly and sustainably, with major indicators placing it in front of other developing countries, giving shape to the largest learning society in which all people can engage in life-long and flexible learning. It will also provide a sound environment for social and human capital, where "everyone will be useful." Third, the strategy to make China strong via the development of human resources will become the core strategy, accelerating the expansion and improvement of China's personnel contingent, giving shape to a new order of personnel at different levels. Finally, China will become more appealing and influential in attracting international talents, realizing a major shift from a brain drain to a brain gain.

---

[8] Personnel contribution refers to the contribution of human capital to economic growth. It is a core input factor in economic operations. It is the share of contributions to economic growth through its own progressive gains and external spillover effect.

Table 5.4 Main indicators of human resource development (2008–2030)

	2008	2015	2020	2030
Aggregate of human resources (10,000)	11,385	15,625	18,025	27,000
R&D personnel per 10,000 labor (person/year)	24.8	33	43	55
% of highly skilled personnel in skilled labor	24.4	27	28	35
% of mainly working age population receiving tertiary education	9.2	15	20	30
% of human capital input in GDP	10.75	13	15	18
Personnel contribution	18.9	32	35	40

Sources: Data for 2008–2020 was sourced from State Medium- and Long-term Human Resources Development Program (2010–2020) -(June 2010); data for 2030 are the estimates of the author

A Strong Power in S&T Innovation

During the mid-1990s, the Chinese government designed a strategy to invigorate the nation via the development of science and technology. This provided a significant impetus to its development and accelerated the pace of China's catch up and improvements to its S&T innovative capacity. Entering the twenty-first century, China has both maintained a high level of economic growth (with the annual average GDP growth reaching 11.1% over the past 10 years) and brought about an explosive growth in the achievements of S&T innovation. China's percentage of the world's aggregate has been steadily increasing and its world ranking has been continuously improving, breaking the monopoly-hold of the West over the world economy, trade patterns, and S&T innovation. China has become a stronger power in S&T innovation. This has manifested itself in the rise of S&T innovation capacity, S&T human capital, S&T input, and S&T markets. China's is expected to become the world's No. 1 in S&T.

The twenty-first century presents a golden age for significant development and prosperity in global science and technology, and it is an opportunity for China to become a world power in science and technology. By 2030, China's prowess in S&T will represent 30% of the world's total, equivalent to that of the United States and EU combined. In addition, China will become the world's No. 1 in terms of the number of research papers patent applications, S&T R&D input, and high-tech product exports.

China boasts the largest number of research papers published in the world,[9] accounting for 25% of total publishing. Since the mid-1990s, the output of S&T research papers in China has rapidly grown. According to the "Global Research

---

[9] Thomson Reuters Web of Science databank has collated the total number of research papers per country and its percentage in the total number of papers published worldwide. This provides an indicator for the S&T innovation capacity of a country. These science papers mainly come from Science Citation Index Expanded (SCI-EXPANDED), Social Sciences Citation Index (SSCI), Arts & Humanities Citation Index (A&HCI).

Table 5.5 Share of research papers of the five major world economies (1980–2030)

Unit: %

	1980	1990	2000	2009	2020	2030
China	0.2	1.3	3.7	10.9	18.0	25.0
USA	39.7	34.9	28.6	29.0	24.0	20.0
EU	32.2	29.6	34.2	36.5	30.0	24.0
Japan	7.2	7.6	9.6	6.7	5.0	4.0
Russia	5.7	6.2	3.3	2.6	2.0	2.0

Sources: Thomson Reuters, Web of Science; Jonathan Adams, Christopher King, Nobuko Miyairi, and David Pendlebury, Global Research Report: Japan, Thomson Reuters Global Research Report Series, 2010; data for 2020 and 2030 are the estimates of the author

Report" released by Thomson Reuters, the number of S&T papers published in China increased from 1,745 in 1981 to 127,075 by 2009, with China's total world percentage rising from 0.4 to 10.9%. Thus, China has become the second largest paper producer in the world after the United States (if the current trend continues, China is expected to overtake the EU within 10 years to become the No. 1) (Adams and Pendlebury 2010). By 2030, the percentage of research papers published by China will reach 25% of the world's total as against 24% by the 27 countries of the EU. This shows the consolidation of China's position as a major innovator and producer of world science and technology (Table 5.5).

In terms of the quality of these research papers,[10] China has made great inroads, advancing steadily up the world ranks. China will rank among the top three countries in terms of the number of citations during the period 2020–2030,[11] advancing toward the No. 1 spot.

China has had the largest number of patent applications in the world. Patent applications reflect the technology innovation capacity of a country. A mature patent system also reflects the degree of maturity of the country's intellectual property rights market. China established its national patent system in 1985. In the ensuing 25 years, it has overtaken the EU and South Korea to become the third largest patent application country.[12] According to Thomson Reuters' Derwent World Patents

---

[10] The quality of a country's papers is usually measured by the number of citations and the world ranking in a given period of time (10 years).

[11] According to SCI databank, in the 10 years from 1994 to 2004, China ranked 18th in the world. In the 10 years from 2000 to 2010, China edged into the top ten (8th), with a average citation for each paper of 5.9. By this trend, China may advance into the top 5 before 2015, ranked 5th. China has realized, 5–7 years ahead of time, the goal set in the Medium- and Long-term Development Program for Science and Technology (2006–2020). Nevertheless, China still has a considerable gap to bridge with advanced countries such as the United States (15.8), the Netherlands (15.3), and the UK (14.7) in terms of the average citations per paper (see China S&T Information Institute: Statistical Result of China's S&T research papers, 2010).

[12] According to data from the World Intellectual Property Right Organization, 4,065 patent applications were registered by domestic residents in 1985, 0.6% of the world's total. By 2008, this figure increased to 194,579, accounting for 18.2% of the world's total.

Table 5.6 Percentages of world total patent applications of the five major economies (1980–2030)

Unit: %

	1980	1990	2000	2008	2020	2030
China		0.9	3.1	18.2	25.0	35.0
USA	12.4	13.4	20.0	21.7	15.0	12.0
EU	19.8	12.5	14.4	10.5	10.0	9.0
Japan	33.1	49.2	46.6	30.9	22.0	17.0
Russia	33.0	16.7	2.8	2.6	2.0	2.0

Note: Data for Russia in 1980–1990 are those of the former Soviet Union
Sources: World Intellectual Property Organization, Intellectual Property Statistics 2010 edition; Data for 2020 and 2030 are the estimates of the author

Index, starting from 2006, China has overtaken Europe and South Korea in the aggregate of patents. Thus, China is on par with South Korea and Europe. China produces 14% of the total patents of the five major economies, while South Korea and Europe produce 12%. China will overtake both the United States and Japan in 2011 (and the United States will exceed Japan by 2013) (Zhou and Stembridge 2010). By 2030, China's share of patent applications by domestic residents will represent 35% of the world's total, close to the combined total of the United States, the EU, and Japan (Table 5.6).

The above results show that China will achieve 10 years ahead of time the goal of reaching the top five in terms of annually authorized creation patents by domestic residents as stated in the national Medium- and Long-term Development Program for Science and Technology (2006–2020). In 2013, China will become the world's No. 1 in terms of the number of authorized creation patents.

China will become the biggest country in terms of S&T input, with its share to reach a quarter of the world's total R&D input. By 2030, the global R&D input is likely to reach 3% of GDP and that of China is expected to reach 2.5–3%, with its share in the world's total to reach 25%, the world's largest R&D input. By comparing the number of research papers and the amount of patent applications, we can determine that China's S&T input with regard to the world's total is still relatively low (Table 5.7).

China has become the world's No. 1 in high-tech exports.[13] According to data from the EU Commission, China overtook the EU in 2006 to become the biggest high-tech exporter in the world. In 2006, China's high-tech exports represented 16.9% of the world's exports while those of the United States, EU, and Japan were 16.8, 15.0 and 8.0%, respectively (Meri 2009).By 2020, China's high-tech exports will make up 25% of the world's total, exceeding the combined total of the United States and the EU. By 2030, the percentage will further rise to 30% (Table 5.8).

---

[13] High-tech products refer to those with high R&D intensity, such as aerospace, computer, medicine, scientific instruments and meters, and electronic equipment. The definitions are similar to World Development Indicators, OECD High-Tech Statistics and Pavitt's Taxonomy (Martin Srholec 2007).

China will become the No. 1 power in science and technology, equal to that of the United States and EU combined. By S&T power, we refer to the comprehensive capacity of S&T innovation (see Box 5.2). S&T competition is in essence competition in all areas of science and technology. The period 2010–2030 will be characterized by China's rapid increase in S&T authority. China will overtake the United States to become the No. 1 S&T power in 2015. By 2020, China's share of the world's total S&T power will reach 23.2%, far exceeding that of the United States, and 30% by

---

Box 5.2 How to Measure S&T Power

In 2008, we put forward the term science and technology (S&T) power. It refers to the capacity of using various national and international S&T resources. S&T power is measured by the percentage of S&T capacities (i.e., scientific innovative, technology innovative, the use of new technologies, obtaining global information, and R&D investment) reflected in the world totals for five specific indicators (the number of papers published in international S&T publications, the amount of creation patent applications by domestic residents, the number of PCs in use, the number of Internet users, and R&D spending to calculate the S&T power by the method of equal weights) (Angang Hu and Xiong Yizhi 2011). The indicators used to measure the innovative capacity of a country (according to the framework of the OECD) should include (1) input, including capital input, such as R&D spending and venture capital as well as human resources inputs such as R&D personnel and tertiary school graduates; (2) output, including direct R&D output, such as high-tech products (export), new products and technological processes, scientific research papers and patents, as well as other economic and social outputs such as job creation, productivity, and sectorial spillover effect; and (3) input–output media, including technology market, and S&T parks and incubators (Schaaper 2009). Any indicator, aggregate, and per capita value can present two different pictures of China's innovation system. Although each has its own implications, the per capita indicator is often misleading and difficult to reflect the regional innovative activities, because China's innovative activities are more active than those of other OECD member countries. Even the innovative activities of just a few provinces in China exceed those of OECD member countries (OECD 2008). Thus, we have adjusted the method to calculate S&T power. We have selected five indicator categories that reflect scientific innovation capacity, technology innovation capacity, S&T human capital, S&T input capacity, and S&T market capacity and use them to calculate the percentage of major countries in the world's total and use the equal weight method to arrive at the S&T power.[14]

---

[14] The five indicators are (1) number of paper published in international publications, (2) amount of creation patent applications by domestic residents, (3) number of R&D scientists and engineers, (4) R&D and experiment expenditure and (5) export of high-tech products.

Table 5.7 Percentages of world total R&D spending of the five major economies (1980–2030)

Unit: %

	1981	1990	2000	2009	2020	2030
China	1.3	1.7	2.9	12.1	18.0	25.0
USA	26.6	36.1	29.4	29.8	25.0	20.0
EU	24.8	35.0	21.5	23.6	20.0	20.0
Japan	8.6	15.7	10.7	11.8	9.0	7.0
Russia	8.6	6.8	1.3	1.9	1.5	1.5

Note: (1) GDP is calculated using PPP (2005 international dollars); (2) GDP data for Russia 1981 and 1985 are estimated using data from the former Soviet Union, 1981 and 1985; (3) data for China 1981–1990 are the percentage of fiscal funding of R&D in GDP

Sources: Data for China were sourced from the State Statistical Bureau, Statistical data 60 years of New China, China Statistical Yearbook, 2010; data for USA, Japan, and Russia for 1981–1990 were sourced from the OECD, OECD Factbook 2005; data for 1995–2005 were sourced from the OECD, OECD Factbook 2010; data for Russia 1981–1990 are those of the former Soviet Union, from NSF, Science and Engineering Indicators 2000; data for the EU for 1995–2009 were sourced from EuroStat, European Commission; data for the USA and Russia for 2009 are those of 2008, from NSF, Science and Engineering Indicators 2010; data for Japan for 2009 were sourced from Survey of Research & Development, Japan Statistics Bureau & Statistics Center; GDP data were sourced from the World Bank, World Development Indicator 2010; data from 2020 to 2030 are the estimates of the author

Table 5.8 Percentage of world total high-tech exports of the five major economies (1980–2030)

Unit: %

	1980	1990	2000	2008	2020	2030
China	0.03	0.6	3.7	19.7	25.0	30.0
USA	26.1	22	19.6	13.4	10.0	8.0
EU	24.7	20.2	16.1	13.1	10.0	8.0
Japan	15.2	15	11.5	6.4	5.0	4.0
Russia	3.3	0.3	0.4	0.3	1.0	1.0

Note: High-tech products refers to aerospace, computer, office automation equipment, electronics and telecom products, pharmaceuticals, scientific instruments and meters, electrical equipment, electrical machinery and non-electrical machinery

Sources: data for 1995–2008 were sourced from the World Bank, World Development Indicator 2010; data for 1980–1990 are the estimates by the author based on UN Comtrade Database, among which data for Russia 1980 and 1985 are estimates based on data for the former Soviet Union; data for 2020 and 2030 are the estimates of the author

2030, which is equal to its share of the world's total economic aggregate (Table 5.9). On the one hand, China's economic power will stimulate a rise in S&T power; on the other hand, the rise of China's S&T power will act as an important motivating force for sustainable economic development.

Table 5.9 Science & technology power of the five major economies (1980–2030)

Unit: %

	1980	1990	2000	2010	2020	2030
China	2.3	2.9	5.4	16.1	23.2	30.0
USA	24.6	25.0	22.8	22.7	17.8	14.4
EU	24.2	22.6	20.4	20.8	17.0	15.2
Japan	16.5	20.5	18.1	14.1	10.2	8.0
Russia	12.2	7.5	2.7	2.8	2.3	2.3
China/USA (time)	0.10	0.12	0.24	0.71	1.30	2.08
China/USA+EU (time)	0.05	0.06	0.13	0.37	0.67	1.01

Source: Tables 5.5, 5.6, 5.7, 5.8 and 5.9

Strongest IT Development Power in the World

Global IT development has become an irreversible trend in the twenty-first century. An IT infrastructure provides the basic conditions for a country's IT development. Just as railway, highways, and power grids have played key roles in the previous two industrial revolutions, IT infrastructure has become an indispensable part of production and modern life. As a latecomer in the information society, China has rapidly lifted its IT development levels through the import and utilization of foreign information technology. In addition, it has become a producer and exporter of information development technology, via assimilation and re-innovation. Thus, China has completed its processes of catch-up and overtaking in the global drive for IT development; it has developed from an apprentice to leader in IT development.

In the 1980s, China was a typical marginalized country in terms of IT development. However, in the 1990s it became an active user of IT products and an energetic participant in IT development. At that time, there was a big gap in ICT usage between China and the United States. In 1990, the number of mobile phone users in the United States was 288.4 times that of China and the number of Internet users was 1,515 times greater. However, the gap began to rapidly narrow. China has not only realized its catch-up objectives but has also left the United States far behind. It has already become a potential leader in global IT development.

The number of fixed-phone users in China in 2003 reached 260 million, ranking first in the world. The phone penetration rate in 2009 reached 79.9%. The number of mobile phone users exceeded that of the United States in 2004 and the figure for 2009 was 2.6 times that of the United States. China will have the capacity of bringing fixed-phone coverage to every family by 2030, with the total number of fixed phones likely to reach 350 million. In 2000, China produced 19.2% of the world's computers; in 2005, the percentage reached 83.5%, securing a No. 1 world ranking. By 2007, the China's Internet users exceeded the United States to become No. 1 in the world. By the end of December 2010, the number reached 457 million, including 303 million mobile netizens, ranking first in the world, with the Internet penetration rate rising to 34.3% (China Internet Information Center 2011), higher than the world

Table 5.10 World total percentage of main IT indicators for china and the United States (1990–2030)

	1990	2000	2009	2020	2030
% of world's total mobile phones in					
China	0.2	11.4	16.0	20.0	25.0
USA	46.1	14.6	6.1	5.0	4.0
USA/China (time)	288.40	1.28	0.38	0.25	0.16
% of world's total Internet users in					
China	0.1	5.8	22.9	30.0	35.0
USA	75.8	31.7	16.8	12.0	9.0
USA/China (time)	1515.00	5.51	0.73	0.40	0.26

Sources: Number of mobile phones was sourced from the World Bank, 2006, Information and Communication for Development 2006, The World Bank, p. 42; data for 1990–2009 were sourced from China State Statistical Bureau: "China Statistical Abstract (2010)", p.160, Beijing, China Statistical Press, 2010; the number of Internet users was sourced from "China Statistical Abstract (2010)", p.160, Beijing, China Statistical Press, 2010; data for Internet users of the United States and world come from CIA, The World Factbook, 2011; data for 2020 and 2030 are the estimates of the author

average. By 2030, all Chinese citizens may have access to the Internet (Table 5.10). China will complete the construction of the largest broadband, infused, secure, and omnipresent next generation IT infrastructure, covering super-speed, large capacity, and highly intelligent mobile telecom, Internet, digital TV, and satellite telecom networks.

Thus, China will become a global IT innovative power between 2010 and 2030, possessing the world's largest IT infrastructure and information society.

Summary: China Will Be a Strong Innovative World Power

Mao Zedong drew the roadmap for China's S&T innovation as early as December 1964 when he said that "China should not follow the beaten track of other countries in technology development, crawling along at a snail's pace behind others and that China must break away with conventions and adopt advanced technologies as far as possible and build China into a strong modernized socialist country in not too long a historical period" (Mao Zedong 1999). Mao Zedong opposed "crawlism" in technology development and advocated "leaping forward" or "leapfrogging." However, when Mao Zedong made the above comments, the opportunities and conditions of today were not available to realize his dreams.

After the reform and opening up, China pioneered a unique path regarding S&T innovations, a path that has led to the use of S&T innovations in three ways: re-innovation on the basis of direct imports; imitations to meet the market demand; and the design of new technologies. China has through importation, imitation, innovation, and moving forward, been successful in its transition from a big power in human resources, qualified personnel, and an innovative country, to a strong power in human resources, qualified personnel, and S&T innovation. When viewed from a human resources perspective, China will boast the largest human resources in the world by 2030, enjoying full human resource and employment dividends, and effectively offsetting the adverse impact of the expiration of population dividends. When viewed with regard to the resources of qualified personnel, China will boast the largest contingent of qualified personnel with Chinese characteristics, which will include not only top-end researchers but also a workforce with practical skills and experts in the areas of practical technologies. When viewed from the perspective of S&T power, China will stand at the top of the world in terms of major S&T output, with higher quality S&T products, and science and technology to become the foremost motivating power propelling the economy forward. In a word, China's quantitative indicators of human resources, qualified personnel resources, and S&T power will, by and large, be equal to that of the United States and the EU combined to become the S&T innovation center of the world.

References

Adams J, Pendlebury D (2010) Global research report: United States. Thomson Reuters global research report series

Angang Hu, Xiong Yizhi (2011) Quantitative assessment of China's science and technology power (1980–2004). Tsinghua University Gazette (Philosophy and Social Sciences Edition) 23(2):104–119

Barro R, Jong-Wha Lee (2010) A new data set of educational attainment in the world, 1950–2010. NBER Working paper no. 15902, Cambridge

China Internet Information Center (CNNIC) (2011) 27th Internet Development Report of China 29 Jan 2011.

Hu Jintao (2011) Speech at the meeting in celebration of the 100th Founding Anniversary of Tsinghua University, 24 Apr 2011

Mao Zedong (1996) Manuscripts of Mao Zedong since the Founding of China, vol 11. Central Documentation Press, Beijing, p 272

Mao Zedong (1999) Build China into a modern, powerful socialist country, December 1964. In: Collected writings of Mao Zedong, vol 8. People's Publishing House, Beijing, p 341

Meri T (2009) China passes the EU in high-tech exports. EuroStat Stat Focus (No. 25/2009)

OECD (2008) OECD reviews of innovation policy: China. OECD, Paris, pp 46–50

Schaaper M (2009) Measuring China's innovation system: national specificities and international comparisons. OECD science, Technology and industry working papers, 2009/1, Paris

Srholec M (2007) High-tech exports from developing countries: a symptom of technology Spurtsor statistical illusion? Review of World Economics 143(2):2007

Zhou E, Stembridge B (2010) Patented in China: the present and future state of innovation in China. Thomas Reuters, Philadelphia

Chapter 6
High-Welfare State

Man appropriates his comprehensive essence in a
comprehensive manner, that is to say, as a whole man.

Marx (1844)

The fundamental aim of China's development is to improve the welfare of its population, providing not only a prosperous and decent life for all, but also higher levels of education, and a healthier and longer life.

Hu Jintao's report to the 17th National Party Congress pointed out that, "We must do our best to ensure that all our people enjoy their rights to education, employment, medical and old-age care, and housing" (Hu Jintao 2007).

Over the past 60 years, especially the 30 years since the reform and opening up, China has created the largest miracle in human history, which is reflected not only in the dramatic speed of development but also in the progress achieved in human development. China is one of the countries with the greatest improvement in its human development index (HDI). The UN Human Development Report 2010 pointed out that China ranks second following Oman among the top movers in HDI in the past 40 years (1970–2010) (UNDP 2010).

The concept of "People first and shared wealth" continues from income-centered development to high-welfare development. It requires a change in the GDP-centered measuring method, which produces "GDP growth without improvement in national happiness." Joseph Stiglitz once described the phenomenon of the GDP indicator as having nothing to do with real social welfare, with positive economic indicators masking the social reality of "wealth full of poverty."[1] This chapter puts forward the

---

[1] In 1990, UNDP developed the human development index (HDI) to measure the achievements of a country in three basic dimensions of human development: a long and healthy life (life expectancy at birth); access to knowledge (mean years of schooling and expected years of schooling); and a decent standard of living (GNI per capita) (PPP US$). HDI includes per capita GDP, so it is better than a simple per capita GDP. The index is rich in content, with clear meaning, and is therefore highly recognized and broadly accepted.

A. Hu et al., *China 2030*, DOI 10.1007/978-3-642-31328-8_6,
© Springer-Verlag Berlin Heidelberg 2014

idea of using national happiness to measure development in reference to the UNDP human development concept. A high-welfare state has four indicators: high income, high education, high health, and high human development. In order to achieve real measurement, we have developed the gross human development index (GHDI) based on HDI to replace GDP as a measure of real national wealth. While GDP indicates economic wealth, high national happiness also measures shared wealth and the popularization of basic public services (Chap. 7), reflecting the indicators of a country's sustainable development capacity (Chap. 8). Please note, this book does not include measures of material living and life satisfaction (which includes a subjective view of happiness).

Thus, what are China's human development achievements as represented in education and health? How do we interpret the relationship between human development and the rise of China? What are the human development trends for the next 20 years? This chapter presents an outline for the next 20 years. China will become a country with high welfare development, not only entering the ranks of high-income countries but also becoming a country with high levels of education, health, and human development. China will also have the highest GHDI, which will be more than three times that of the United States.

High-Income Country

The development level of a country or region is usually measured by per capita income or per capita GDP. The World Bank measures economic development levels using per capita gross national income. It divides countries into low-income, lower-middle income, upper-middle income, and high-income countries. However, China adopts per capita GDP to categorize development stages: poverty stage with less than US$400; adequate food and clothing stage with US$400–800; toward a wealthy or prosperous stage with US$800–3,000; an affluent or wide-ranging prosperous stage with US$3,000–8,000 dollars; and high-income stage or very wealthy stage with more than US$8,000 dollars.

According to data provided by Angus Maddison, in the 188 years from 1820 to 2008, the per capita GDP of the UK grew 13.5 times, Germany 19.3 times, the United States 24.8 times, and Japan 34.3 times. This was a unique period of the capitalist era in human history, in which such economies developed at a high speed. It proved that the "economic growth of capitalist countries was stronger than that of non-capitalist countries" (McCraw 2006).

At the beginning of the reform and opening up in China, the per capita gross national income (GNI) was less than US$300, making it a low-income country by World Bank measurements. By 1998, per capita GNI topped US$800 to reach the lower-middle income level; in 2009, the figure was US$3,650, still at the lower-middle level but already reaching the average of middle-income countries (US$3,373 in 2009) and close to upper-middle levels (US$3,946 at the lower end in 2009). This shows that economic growth under socialism in China is stronger and faster than the aforementioned economic growth within capitalist countries.

Table 6.1 China's GDP and per capita GDP growth index and average annual growth (1978–2030)

	1978	2010	2020	2030	1978–2010 Annual growth (%)	2010–2030 Annual growth (%)	1978–2030 Annual growth (%)
GDP	1.00	20.57	44.4	87.4	9.9	7.5	9.0
Per capita GDP	1.00	14.71	30.3	62.5	8.8	7.0	8.3

Note: data calculated using the constant price method
Sources: data for 1978–2010 were sourced from the State Statistical Bureau: "China Statistical Abstract 2011", p. 23, China Statistical Press, 2011. Data for 2010 and beyond are the estimates of the author

We estimate that China's GDP growth will remain at 7–8% from 2010 to 2030 (Chap. 4). As China's population records zero growth (below 2%), China's per capita GDP growth will remain at 7% or higher, which is 1.8 percentage points less than for 1978–2010. Up to 2030, China's per capita GDP will be 4.2 times that of 2010 and 62.5 times that of 1978 (Table 6.1).

In the next 20 years, China will move from a prosperous level to a wealthy level, realizing ahead of time the goal of a prosperous society for all. Globally, China's current economic and social development levels belong in the middle-income level and are moving from the lower-middle income level to the upper-middle income level. China will enter the upper-middle income level during the first year of the 12th Five-year Plan period to become a para-high income country before 2020 and a high-income country by 2030, basically realizing its goal of modernization.

In this chapter, we have adopted three methods to calculate the US dollar value of per capita GDP from 2010 to 2030 and the catch up coefficient of China's per capita GDP vis-à-vis United States per capita GDP. The first is the exchange rate method or market exchange rate method, taking into account China's nominal GDP average deflator and the changes in the exchange rate of the RMB to the dollar; the second is the PPP current price method adopted by the World Bank, taking into account the changes in the dollar price; the third is the PPP constant price adopted by Maddison, with the 1990 international dollar price as the benchmark.

No matter what method is used, the results unanimously indicate a convergence in the following decades. China's per capita GDP was 2.6–11.7% that of the United States in 2000; up to 2010 the percentage was 10–25%; and by 2020, it will be 25–40%, which means China will be in for a para-high income period. By 2030, China's per capita GDP will be about half that of the United States,[2] representing China's entry into the high-income stage (Table 6.2)

---

[2] This method is different from the method used by economists, which measures the dollar value of per capita GDP using constant price and constant exchange rate methods. The use of the exchange rate method underestimates the real purchasing power of RMB and accompanied with economic globalization and integration, the exchange rate of the RMB to the dollar will assume an upward trend. Therefore, using the exchange rate method, the dollar value of China's per capita GDP would move to a long-term convergence toward PPP current price and PPP constant price. By2030, the dollar value of China's per capita GDP would be approximately 50% of the United States according to the various methods of calculation.

Table 6.2 Dollar value of China's per capita GDP and catch up coefficient relative to the US (2000–2030)

		2000	2010	2015	2020	2025	2030
Per capita GDP (US dollar)							
Exchange rate	China	925	4,249	8,220	16,025	27,255	46,670
(current price)	USA	35,040	47,390	55,360	64,838	76,177	89,798
PPP (current price)	China	2,305	7,164	11,137	17,448	25,063	36,246
(World Bank)	USA	35,040	46,626	50,554	54,955	59,926	65,566
PPP (1990 price)	China	3,335	7,822	10,748	14,883	18,896	24,153
(Maddison)	USA	28,433	30,589	33,166	36,053	39,314	43,014
Catch up coefficient (USA = 100)							
Exchange rate method		2.6	9.0	14.8	24.7	35.8	52.0
(current price)							
PPP (current price)		6.6	15.4	22.0	31.8	41.8	55.3
(World Bank)							
PPP (1990 price)		11.7	25.6	32.4	41.3	48.1	56.2
(Maddison)							

Note: (1) Catch up coefficient = China's per capita GDP/United States per capita GDP × 100; (2) for the GDP aggregate calculated using the exchange rate method, 2010–2020, China's GDP real growth will be 8%, GDP deflator will be 3%, appreciation of RMB to the dollar will be 3%, United States GDP real growth will be 2%, and GDP deflator will be 2%; for 2020–2030, China's GDP real growth will be 7%, GDP deflator will be 2%, appreciation of RMB to the dollar will be 2%, United States GDP real growth will be 2%, GDP deflator will be 2%; (3) for the GDP aggregate calculated using the PPP current price method, 2010–2030, the GDP deflator will be 2.5%; (4) for the GDP aggregate calculated using the PPP constant price, 2010–2020, China's GDP growth will be 7%, and for 2020–2030, China's GDP growth will be 5%; United States GDP growth will be 2.5% for 2010–2030
Sources: World Bank, World Development Indicator 2011; Angus Maddison, Statistics on World Population, GDP and Per Capita GDP, 1–2008 AD, 2010, http://www.ggdc.net/MADDISON/oriindex. htm; Population Division of the Department of Economic and Social Affairs of the United Nations Secretariat, World Population Prospects: The 2010 Revision, http://esa.un.org/unpd/wpp/index.htm

By 2030, China's per capita GDP will reach US$40,000 to enter the ranks of developed countries, far beyond the goal set by Deng Xiaoping for the middle of the twenty-first century. Deng Xiaoping conceived that up to the middle of the twenty-first century, per capita GDP would reach US$4,000 to rank among the middle-income developed countries. He said, "It means that by the middle of the next century we hope to reach the level of the middle-income developed countries. If we can achieve this goal, first, we shall have accomplished a tremendous task; second, we shall have made a real contribution to mankind; and third, we shall have demonstrated more convincingly the superiority of the socialist system" (Deng Xiaoping 1993).

By 2020, China will have accomplished this goal, reaching the middle-income developed level ahead of time. By 2030, China will have also accomplished its basic modernization ahead of time. We have every reason to believe that China's per capita GDP will be close to that of the United States and realize complete modernization by the middle of the century.

What requires further explaining is that calculations using per capita GDP underestimates China's real economic and social development levels. We need an indicator that more closely reflects the real situation, such as Engel's coefficient. We estimate that by 2030, the Engel's coefficient of China's urban and rural households will drop to below 30% (see section "Common Wealth Shared by both Urban and Rural Areas" of Chap. 7) to enter a new wealthier stage and the living areas of urban and rural residents will reach the level that took developed countries 100 years to achieve,[3] but will be more substantial and comfortable than many developed countries. In addition, we need more important development indicators such as education, health, and human development to measure China's level of social development and development trends.

High Education Levels

Chinese Premier Wen Jiabao once pointed out that, "The whole world is talking about the 'rise of China'. But what people talk most about is GDP, I think the 'rise of China' lies in qualified personnel and in education."[4] "**Education is the foundation of people's livelihood.** Only when education is flourishing, is it possible for the country to flourish. Education is the best way for the economy to develop and the country to prosper. It provides the basic conditions and methods for the world's most populated country to become strong. The twenty-first century is the century of the rejuvenation of the great Chinese nation and the golden age for the development of modern education and human resources. It is now that China's transition will occur, from a notable power in education and human resources, to a dominant power. Only when the Chinese people are in the process of modernization, is it possible for human capital to develop in leaps and bounds, releasing their creativity. Only then, we can say that a large population is an extremely good thing." China's population will no longer be a heavy burden on development but its biggest foundation; it will no longer be a disadvantage, which holds back development, but its biggest advantage; and it will no longer be a liability for development but its biggest asset. The fundamental purpose of the socialist revolution in China over the past 60 years, especially the reform and opening up, is the investment in human capital, to release the productivity of the greatest labor force in the world, and to display the creativity of the greatest number of qualified personnel (Box 6.1).

---

[3] The per capita living area of urban residents in 2010 reached 31.6 square meters and that of rural areas, 34.1 square meters (State Statistical Bureau 2010). The average per capita living area of high-income countries is 376 square feet (37 square meters) and that of upper-middle income countries such as Greece, South Korea, and Spain is 236 square feet (approx. 23 square meters) (Qiao Lei 2010).

[4] Renmin Net, Beijing, Feb. 27, 2011.

Box 6.1 Index of Human Welfare

The current index system for measuring wealth has undergone three major stages.

A great humanitarian invention of the twentieth century was the GDP accounting system (the first stage). It was the first time in history that a comparative scientific method was used to evaluate the wealth of a country or a region. However, reviews of GDP identified a number of drawbacks such as inadequate understanding, knowledge, and information. At the beginning of the 1990s, a green GDP was created to eliminate the limitations of the original GDP measure. Green GDP takes into account the cost of human development, especially ecological costs.

In the 1990s, a further great invention appeared: the human development index (HDI), which has become an important index to measure national development levels worldwide. HDI does not only take into consideration per capita GDP but also indicators such as education and health. Based on this index, the author put forward in 2003 the concept of GHDI, which represents HDI multiplied by total population. GHDI provides a more scientific measure of human wealth. Using this index, the author carried out comparative studies of China with the United States and India. The process of GDP to green GDP and then to GHDI constitutes the second stage of the index system.

Despite this reform, there is still inadequate understanding, knowledge, and information with regard to human wealth. The creation of the gross national happiness (GNH) measure is the third innovation or stage. With the understanding of wealth progressing through three stages, from GDP to green GDP, and then to GHDI, and finally to GNH, the concept of human wealth is becoming closer to its ideal. Of course, this is only in relative terms. It was some time before the term GNH was developed. It is not only a new concept but has its own index and computing method. We believe that one day GNH will be accepted worldwide.

What is the meaning of the 'people-centered' concept? It can be defined as the maximization of economic net welfare or the maximization of social welfare (from an economics or sociology perspective) to further improve green GDP or GHDI. However, this definition is not sufficient, as it does not reflect spiritual and cultural aspects. The scientific approach to development and the people-centered concept seeks to explore how to make people happier and how to maximize happiness under the limitations of external constraints. Thus, the approach to happiness embodies the same scientific approach as that to development. GNH may help us to renew our understanding of what development is and what happiness is, to increase the happiness levels of people living in middle-income development countries. Even as we ascend to the high-income level, the happiness of the people will remain at the heart of development.

GNH is, in reality, identical to China's idea of harmony. Harmony and happiness have the same goal. China may well carry out re-innovation as it is only by building harmonious families, communities, enterprises, regions, and countries and even a harmonious world, that happiness can be achieved.

Table 6.3 Average years of schooling in China, the United States, and the world, and China's catch up coefficient relative to the United States (1950–2030)

Year	China	USA	World	China/USA (%)
1950	1.0	8.38	3.17	11.9
1960	2.0	9.15	3.65	21.9
1970	3.2	10.77	4.45	29.7
1980	5.33	12.03	5.29	44.3
1990	6.43	12.14	6.09	53.0
2000	7.85	12.71	6.98	61.8
2010	9.0	12.2	7.76	73.8
2020	10.0	12.3	8.5	81.3
2030	12.0	12.5	9.2	96.0

Sources: data for the USA and world for 1950–2010 were sourced from Barro and Jong-Wha Lee (2010); data for China for 1950–2010 are the estimates of the author; data for 2020–2030 are the estimates of the author

The biggest change in China's socialist modernization over the past 60 years has been modernization itself. That is, the constant rise in the level of modernization factors, for example human capital (average years of schooling, skills and experience, specialization, and health). It is the largest-scale change the world has seen. In 2010, the average years of education received by Chinese nationals was 9 years, 9 times that of 1949 when the New China was founded, and already higher than the world average (7.76 years). China's average years of schooling in 1949 was only 11.9% that of the United States; by 2010, it was 78.3%. China has completed a historical transition from a notable power with a huge population to a dominant power in human resources. It has popularized compulsory education, with the net enrolment at primary schools reaching 99.4% in 2009, 99.0% at junior middle school, and 79.2% at senior middle school. Attendance numbers at universities rank first in the world, and may exceed 83% by 2015. Tertiary education has transitioned from elite education to popular education, with gross enrolments reaching 24.2% in 2009. By 2015, they could reach more than 30%. China has engaged in a catapult transition from the most populated country characterized by illiteracy, ignorance, and backwardness (the 'sick man of East Asia') to a dominant power in human resources and qualified personnel resources (Table 6.3).

China is facing multi-faceted challenges in its educational development. The current education supply is far from satisfying the huge demand by the people in terms of quality, diversification, and individualization. While China has solved the problem of providing enough education opportunities, the quality of the education could be improved. The quality of China's education resources is falling short of demand as China has an educational system with limited public education resources. China's educated population makes up approximately 20% of the world's total. However, its GDP (exchange rate method) accounted for only 5.9% of the world's total in 2007 and the public educational expenditure accounted for just 4.2%. These rates are low because China's percentage of public education spending in GDP (3.2%)

was lower than the world's total in world total GDP (4.5%).[5] The current educational system, teaching methods, and training model are flawed, as the only purpose appears to be boosting the enrolment rates of universities. In addition, the system is unable to adapt to the needs of the employment market and international competition, nor accommodate the diversity of its students. Furthermore, the current urban/rural education divide is huge. Compulsory education service levels vary greatly from region to region and education opportunities are unequal and unfair among different schools and groups. A considerable number of teachers do not meet national standards, directly affecting the quality of education. The gross enrolment rates for China's three-year preschool education are very low (47.3% in 2008).

In the next 20 years, China has to effectively address the current issues facing education reform and development. By 2030, China will have to realize the modernization of China's unique education system and build a learning society in which all people can engage in life-long and flexible learning. With the achievement of this, China will become a dominant power in human resources. This is an ambitious strategic goal. It requires the transformation China's population burden into an advantageous and competitive element of human resources. In addition, China's education system will need to transform from a notable power to a dominant power by developing and using the world's largest, richest, and most valuable personnel resources. It entails the training of hundreds of millions of specialized personnel and educated laborers; it entails the expansion of learning opportunities for all, investments in human capital, improvements in the development capabilities of all people, and the building of a learning society.

By 2030, China's major education development indicators will reach or approach the levels of developed countries. The realization of modernization in education will satisfy China's growing demand. Thus, the fundamental aims of education reform and development will have been met. One of the key objectives of socialist modernization is to create a learning society possessing distinctly Chinese characteristics. Education is vital to ensure a prosperous population and a strong country. Therefore, it is necessary to accelerate China's development of continuing education and to establish a variety of learning organizations, as well as a flexible and open life-long educational system. China using such characteristics, will build the world's largest learning society in which "everybody learns anywhere and anytime" so that all of China's population can "have educational opportunities, achieve good results in learning and apply what they learn." An educated population will provide the human resources to increase China's comprehensive national power. Human resources are the basis of human capital to increase China's comprehensive national power and to use numerous strategic resources. Human capital will play a special and long-term role in China's development. In this sense, of all resources, human capital is the most precious just as Mao Zedong stated.[6] As seen in international comparisons, if the total human capital is the working age population multiplied by average years of

---

[5] Data source: World Bank, World Development Indicators 2009, pp. 14–16, 80–82.

[6] Mao Zedong said, "Of all things in the world, people are the most precious" (Mao Zedong 1949).

schooling, then China accounts for one-quarter of the world's total. Thus, China enjoys the utmost competitive advantage in human resources. China will have the biggest comparative advantage in terms of international cooperation and international competition.

By 2020 we estimate that the gap between China and the United States regarding expected years of schooling will narrow from 4.4 years (2009) to 1.2 years. China's expected preschool education years will reach 2.45 years to overtake the United States. The gap between the two countries for higher education will be narrowed from the current 3.2 years to 2.2 years. By 2030, China's expected years of education will reach 17.9 years to overtake the United States and the expected preschool years will reach 2.7 years, 0.8 years more than the United States. The expected years of higher education will reach 3.5 years, narrowing the gap with the United States to 0.9 years. These milestones will mark the completion of China's transition from a notable power in human resources to a dominant power in human resources and qualified personnel (Table 6.4).[7]

A Healthy State

Health is essential for livelihood and it is the foundation of welfare and happiness. Health is the eternal pursuit of man. Thus, Amartya Sen stated, "Health, like education, is among the basic necessities that give value to human life."[8] According to an evaluation of the World Bank, a change in adult health status can result in a 16% gain in hours worked and a 20 % increase in individual income.[9]

China has already controlled traditional diseases, realizing a shift to a modern population development characterized with low birth rates and low infant mortality rates. Life expectancy has increased from approximately 35 years before liberation in 1949 to 68 years in 1978, and 73 years in 2008. It may reach 74 years by 2010 (CIA 2010). Pregnancy and maternal mortality rates in China dropped from 1,500/100,000 in the 1950s to 34.2/100,000 by 2008. Infant mortality rates dropped from 200 to 11 % by 2008, placing China alongside other front-ranking developing countries.[10] As seen in international comparisons, China's improving life expectancy represents its relentless catch up process with the United States. In 1950, the gap

---

[7] In fact, American education lags behind in its economic development level. South Korea's expected years of education from preschool to higher education in 2009 is 18.1 years, 0.7 years more than the United States; its expected years of schooling from primary to higher education is 16.9 years, 0.9 years more than the United States. However, the per capita GDP of South Korea (exchange rate method, current dollar price) is only 37.1 % that of the United States.

[8] Amartya Sen, "Poverty as Capability Deprivation", Chinese edition, "Vision", Issue No. 4.

[9] Human Development Unit, East Asia and Pacific Region, World Bank, "Toward a Healthy and Harmonious Life in China: Stemming the Rising Tide of Non-Communicable Diseases".

[10] Chinese health minister Chen Zhu, September 8, 2009.

Table 6.4 Expected years of schooling for China and the United States (2001–2030)

		2001	2009	2020	2030
Preschool	China	1.1	1.4	2.45	2.7
	USA	1.8	1.7	1.8	1.9
	Gap	0.7	0.3	−0.65	−0.8
Primary-middle	China	9.3	10.3	11.55	11.7
	USA	11.6	11.5	11.5	11.5
	Gap	2.3	1.2	−0.05	−0.2
Higher	China	0.5	1.2	2.25	3.5
	USA	3.3	4.4	4.4	4.4
	Gap	2.8	3.2	2.15	0.9
Primary-higher	China	9.9	11.6	13.8	15.2
	USA	15.4	16	16	16.5
	Gap	5.5	4.4	2.2	1.3
Preschool-high	China	11	13	16.25	17.9
	USA	17.2	17.4	17.4	17.4
	Gap	6.2	4.4	1.15	−0.5

Sources: data for 2001 and 2009 were sourced from UNESCO, Education Database, 2009; data for 2020 and 2030 are the estimates of the author. In the process of calculation, reference was made to the "the State Medium- and Long-term Program for Education Reform and Development (2008–2020)"

between life expectancy rates in the United States and China was 33 years; by 1980 it was narrowed to just 7 years. From 1980 to 2010, the gap was further narrowed to 4.5 years. However, the progress in this period was lower than in the previous period. It took China 30 years to reduce its life expectancy from 67 years to 73.5 years, at a speed equal to that of the United States. It took the United States 30 years to bring its life expectancy from 68 years to 73.6 years (1950–1980). In fact, the mean life expectancy in developed cities such as Shanghai, Beijing, and Hangzhou has already exceeded 80 years, above the average of high-income developed countries (79 years in 2006) (World Bank 2009, Table 1).

However, China still faces various challenges in health development, as the number of people with potentially compromised health grows annually, involving (directly or indirectly) 400 million families and 1.3 billion people. The impact from this growing group is much greater than that brought by other insecurity factors. According to the 2008 4th Health Service Survey, 840 million people do not participate in any sports; 210 million patients have chronic diseases (43 million more than in 2003); and the number of people who regularly consumed alcohol reached 92.60 million.[11] According to an assessment of the World Bank, NCDs (non-communicable disease) are China's number one health threat. They account for 82 % of disease burdens, far exceeding the burdens caused by communicable diseases.[12] China's

---

[11] Statistical Information Center of the Ministry of Public Heal, "Main Results of the Fourth Health Service Survey 2008".

[12] Human Development Unit, East Asia and Pacific Region, World Bank, "Toward a Healthy and Harmonious Life in China: Stemming the Rising Tide of Non-Communicable Diseases".

current smoking population has exceeded 300 million, approximately one-third of the world's total smoking population, and approximately 500 million people have fallen victim to second-hand smoking. The annual death rate due to smoking-associated diseases is close to one million, 12 % of total deaths.[13] In this sense, China is not only most populated country in the world but also a country with the largest diseased population, posing the greatest threat to human health security.

However, China is entering a golden age in terms of health development. From 1949 to 1978, the New China experienced a golden age, completing its first health revolution with the control and elimination of serious communicable diseases and parasitic diseases (a miracle given China's low income level). From 1978 to 2003, China experienced a lower level of development than in the previous golden age, and lagging economic growth. In addition, there was a threat to China's health security with SARS. However, since SARS in 2003, China has shifted its focus to health rather than growth, bringing health development into a new golden age. This golden age will continue for some time to come, seeing both national social and economic development moving to the same progressive track as scientific development.

By 2020, China's mean life expectancy will rise to 77.5 years, with the gap with the United States narrowed from 5 years to 3.1 years. By 2030, it will increase to 80 years, narrowing the gap with the United States to just 1.4 years. China is expected to catch up with and overtake the United States by 2040.

In making these predictions, we have taken into account two development trends. Apart from natural development, there is the trend of planned guidance. China has incorporated its improvements in the mean life expectancy from birth into the 12th Five-year Development Program and has set a goal to increase life expectancy to 74.5 years by 2015 (the author participated in the program's planning process). Guidance by such plans will accelerate the increase of life expectancy. We estimate that by 2020 China's life expectancy should reach 77 years, 1.5 years more than that predicted by the pure trend extrapolation method, reaching the average of developed countries.[14] To attain this goal, government intervention is required to increase the health levels of the middle and western areas of the country, especially rural areas, controlling the incidence of cancer, stroke, heart disease, injuries, poisoning, and perinatal diseases.[15]

Of course, health levels are not only reflected in life expectancy alone, as life expectancy merely represents the length of life but is not a measure of all aspects of health. China's health priorities for its population of more than one billion are to get fit, be more productive, and to live a longer and happier life. In terms of quantitative

---

[13] Speech by Chinese Vice Health Minister Yin Li, XinhuaNet, Beijing, Sept. 18, 2010.

[14] Our estimate is more optimistic than that of the UN and other organizations. According to the new predictions of the UN, China's life expectancy will reach 75.6 years between 2020 and 2025 and up to 77.2 years between 2030 and 2035. See Population Division of the Department of Economic and Social Affairs of the United Nations Secretariat, World Population Prospects: The 2010 Revision· http://esa.un.org/unpd/wpp/index.htm

[15] See Project Group of the Ministry of Public Health, "Healthy China Strategy 2020", Research Report, May 2010.

Table 6.5 Mean Life Expectancy (MLE) and Mean Healthy Life Expectancy (MHLE) of China and the United States (2002–2030)

Unit: years

Country	Indicator	2002	2007	2020	2030
China	MLE	71.1	73	77	80
	MHLE	64.1	66	71	75
	Gap	7	7	6	5
USA	MLE	77.3	78	80.1	81.3
	MHLE	69.3	70	73.1	75.3
	Gap	8	8	7	6
USA/China gap	MLE	6.2	5	3.1	1.3
	MHLE	5.2	4	2.1	0.3

Sources: data for 2002 and 2007 are based on WHO, World Health Statistics, 2005 and WHO, World Health Statistics, 2009; data for 2020 and 2030 are the estimates of the author; data for China for 2020 and 2030 are the estimates of the author in reference to the Project Group of the Ministry of Public Health, Healthy China Strategy 2020 "Research Report", May 2010; data for the USA are based on Population Division of the Department of Economic and Social Affairs of the United Nations Secretariat, World Population Prospects: The 2010 Revision, http://esa.un.org/unpd/wpp/index.htm

indicators, an additional priority is to increase China's mean healthy life expectancy even further. As seen in international comparisons, China's mean healthy life expectancy in 2002 was 64.1 years, 5.8 years less than that of the United States. We estimate that by 2020, China's mean healthy life expectancy will rise to 71 years, narrowing the relative gap with Japan from 10 years to 6.9 years and that with the United States from 4 years to 2.1 years. By 2030, China's mean healthy life expectancy will rise to 75 years, narrowing the relative gap with Japan to 4.4 years and that with the United States to 0.3 years. China is expected to catch up and overtake the United States by 2040 (Table 6.5).

China's health strategy will be carried out in three steps: bringing China's main health indicators up to those of the forerunning developing countries by 2015;developing China to reach the level of middle-income developed countries by 2020, and then the levels of high-income countries by 2030.

China will provide health-for-all basic medical and health services. At the core of China's health development is the realization of the goal of "basic medical and health service for all" set by the 17th National Party Congress. The report stresses that health is the foundation of comprehensive human development. In addition, the report clearly outlines a framework to promote basic medical insurance for workers in cities and towns in an inclusive manner and to provide basic medical insurance for urban residents. It also sets out to establish a variety of new medical systems including a rural cooperative medical service, public health service system, medical service system, medical security system, medicine supply insurance system, and basic medical and health services for all tht covers both urban and rural areas. A planned immunization program will cover 98% of China's children. In addition, over 90% of rural households will have access to tap water by 2020 (compared with just 61% in 2005) and at least 95% by 2030. Thus, China's drinking-water problem will be resolved (previously, more than 300 million rural people, and 80% in the central and western areas, were drinking sub-standard water).[16] Sanitary latrines will be made available for over 80% of the rural population by 2020 (compared with 53.1% in 2005) and will exceed 90% by 2030.

China will also construct an accessible health security system, a basic health care system for both urban and rural residents. This will entail the strengthening of the public health system, carrying out a national health campaign, improving China's emergency response mechanisms and medical rescue systems for disease outbreaks and disasters, and establishing a disease prevention and control system, and a public health and individual health information system. Improvements will be made to China's medical and health service system, with an emphasis on rural three-tier health service networks and a new urban community health service system. A diversified medical service market will be developed to satisfy the health care demands of China's diverse citizens. The rural population will be covered by a primary healthcare social security system, and a medical security system will cover both the urban and rural populations. The government's investent in public health and basic medical services will represent approximately 8 % of the GDP.[17]

China will also seek to establish a health-for-all and fitness-for-all society.[18] This system will improve the health levels of society as a whole. It will include a sports network and a management system with the participation of all citizens, which will be under the guidance of the government but organized by the people. These sports networks will train sports instructors and set up tutoring stations to initiate fitness campaigns. Efforts will be made to carry out various sports and body building activities suitable for mass participation and, therefore, increase the percentage of people participating in sports. The government should advocate a campaign to encourage daily physical exercise for everyone and make the sports and fitness activities more systematic, accessible, and realistic. In addition, the number of people doing regular physical exercise will reach 650 million; China's infant mortality rate will be less than 4 %, and the pregnancy mortality rate of rural women will be reduced to 10/100,000. Efforts1sould also be made to control the spread of AIDS and other communicable diseases (Table 6.6).

A Country with High Human Development

The HDI is a comprehensive index, which includes economy, health, and education. In 1950, China's HDI was 0.225, lower than India's, representing an extremely low level of human development. By 1975, China's HDI had increased to 0.525,

---

[16] Sub-standard drinking water refers to water with high levels of fluoride and arsenic, bitter-tasting, polluted water, water in snail fever-infested areas that have high levels of micro-organisms, and serious water shortages in local areas (Ma Kai 2006).

[17] The percentage of mid-level human development in 2000 was 6.9 % (UNDP 2003).

[18] Jiang Zemin pointed out that "a fairly perfect fitness-for-all and medical and health system will take shape by 2020" (Jiang Zemin 2005).

Table 6.6 China's main health development indicators (2008–2030)

	2008	2015	2020	2030	High-income countries (2007)
Mean life expectancy (years)	73.0	74.5	77.0	80	80
Infant mortality rate (%)	14.9	11	7	4	6
Death rate of children under 5 (%)	18.5	13	8	5	
Pregnancy and maternal death rate (1/100,000)	34	20	16	10	9
Children's immunization rate (%)	90	90	95	98	93

Sources: Project group of the Ministry of Public Health: "Healthy China 2020 Strategy 'Research Report", May 2010; data of high-income countries come from World Bank, World Development indicators 2010; data for 2030 are the estimates of the author

entering lower-middle development levels. According to the new computing method developed by UNDP, China's HDI in 1980 was 0.368, and by 2008 it had increased to 0.663, ranking 86th among 182 countries. China's HDI has experienced the fastest increase of any country, with a mean life expectancy of 72.5 years (and a ranking of 86th), an adult literacy rate of 90.9% (54th), a enrolment rate for the three levels of education of 69.1% (104th); and PPP per capita GDP at US$6,767 (86th).

In 2010, China's HDI was 0.663, at an upper-middle level. The world's HDI was 0.624, belonging to a lower-middle development level. By 2020, global HDI will reach 0.696, close to a high development level and China's will reach 0.750, a high development level. By 2020, in terms of global HDI composition, per capita GDP will reach US$14,000, the average years of schooling will be at 8 years, expected years of schooling will measure 13 years, with a mean life expectancy of 75 years; China's four HDI indicators will be US$14,000, 10 years, 14 years, and 77.5 years, repsectively. By 2030, global HDI will be 0.703, entering the high development stage, while that of China will be 0.776. Between 2040 and 2050, China's HDI is likely to exceed 0.800 to reach the extremely high level. In terms of indicators, the global per capita GDP will reach US$19,000 by 2030, the average years of schooling will reach 9.5 years, the expected years of schooling will reach 14 years, and life expectancy will reach 79 years; China's four indicators will be US$23,000, 10 years, 16 years, and 80 years, respectively.

It took China 25 years to enter the lower-middle development level from the extremely low level. It took a further 20 years to leave that level and enter the upper middle level. By 2015, China will enter a stage of high human development, 20 years time, China will enjoy a period of extremely high human development (Table 6.7).

No matter what method is used, China's per capita GDP by 2030 will be approximately 50% of the United States. However, its HDI will be approximately 85% that of the United States; the gap in life expectancy will be narrowed to only 1.3 years. The expected years of schooling will exceed the United States. This information is useful to determine which level China will reach in the world, and when (it is important to note that the HDI of the United States is not the highest worldwide).

We have introduced the concept of GHDI, which is a country's total population multiplied by HDI. The unit is HDI per person, which reflects the actual total welfare

Table 6.7 HDI for China, the USA, and India and catch up coefficient (1980–2030)

	1980	1990	2000	2005	2010	2020	2030
China	0.368	0.460	0.567	0.616	0.663	0.750	0.776
USA	0.810	0.857	0.893	0.895	0.902	0.919	0.926
India	0.320	0.389	0.440	0.482	0.519	0.559	0.564
China/USA	0.45	0.54	0.63	0.69	0.74	0.82	0.84
India/USA	0.40	0.45	0.49	0.54	0.58	0.61	0.61

Sources: UNDP, Human Development Report 2010; UNDP, Human Development Database; data for 2020 and 2030 are the estimates of the author

Table 6.8 GHDI of China, the United States, and India (1980–2030)

Unit: 100 million HDI

	1980	1990	2000	2005	2010	2020	2030
China	3.62	5.27	7.2	8.05	8.91	10.28	10.84
India	2.24	3.4	4.64	5.5	6.36	7.75	8.59
USA	1.86	2.17	2.52	2.66	2.8	3.1	3.35
China/USA (times)	1.94	2.43	2.85	3.03	3.18	3.36	3.23
India/USA (times)	1.2	1.57	1.84	2.07	2.27	2.5	2.56

Sources: UNDP, Human Development Report 2010; UNDP, Human Development Database; data for 2020–2030 are the estimates of the author

of a country's nationals. If this indicator is used, China's GHDI was already 1.94 times that of the United States in 1980. In 1990 it was 2.43 times that of the United States. Between 2010 and 2030, China's GHDI will be three times that of the United States, higher than the ratio of economic aggregate between the two countries. By 2030, China's GHDI will be 3.23 times that of the United States, and although India will overtake China in population, its GHDI will only be 2.56 times that of the United States (Table 6.8).

If classified using GHDI sources, China's GHDI growth has experienced three stages. The first stage was realized by China's population growth; the second stage was realized by the growth of per capita GDP; and the third stage was realized by the rise in education levels and mean life expectancy. These three stages are in line with the three stages of Confucius, "populous state, affluent state and education." Confucianism is an important historical and cultural source of China's development.

Most countries increase their GHDI by relying on the growth of the total population; however, China has achieved the same by relying on an increase in HDI. China's HDI growth between 1950 and 1975 contributed to 62.08% of GHDI growth. It reduced- somewhat to 50.86% between 1975 and 2000. However, it is expected to be as high as 61.21% between 2000 and 2030. In contrast, India has increased its GHDI by relying on the growth of total population. Its lowest level was 50.19% for 1950–1975. From 1975 to 2000 GHDI remained at a high level of 60% and this will remain constant for 2000–2030. However, the corresponding contribution of HDI growth to GHDI growth has remained at 40%, a relatively low level.

Table 6.9 Contributing factors to China's GHDI (1980–2030)

Unit: %

	Population	Income	Education	Health	Interactive items
1980–1990	36.1	43.8	12.3	3.3	4.5
1990–2000	29.6	39.8	20.3	6.1	4.3
2000–2010	24.8	45.3	21.9	6.0	1.9
2010–2020	22.6	27.3	38.4	9.7	2.1
2020–2030	7.0	45.4	40.4	7.6	−0.3

Sources: UNDP, Human Development Report 2010; UNDP, Human Development Database; data for 2020–2030 are the estimates of the author

More than half a century ago, Mao Zedong commented, "Of all things in the world, people are the most precious. Under the leadership of the Communist Party, as long as there are people, every kind of miracle can be performed (Table 6.9)."

Summary: Toward a High-Level Human Welfare State

Health is the base of human welfare; education is the foundation; and wealth is what human welfare needs. The fundamental aim of development is to improve the welfare of the people. GDP only represents the economic wealth of a country; GHDI is the real wealth. It includes the economic wealth represented by GDP and, and more importantly, the welfare of the people itself, their health and education, which represent social equity.

Since its founding, the United States has spent 234 years (1776–2010) making itself the most developed and wealthiest nation in the world. During that period, China has been increasingly lagging behind and becoming weaker. By 1950, its per capita GDP had reduced from US$600 to US$448, becoming the poorest "sick man of East Asia."[19]

China's per capita income did not begin to grow until after the founding of the New China. This clearly indicated that China really could catch up to the United States and truly create a miracle by increasing the welfare of its people in a relatively short period. It also proved the superiority of the socialist system. From 1949 to 1977, China created its first miracle in human welfare. Under extremely low income per capita, China effected a relatively quick development of its education and health systems, and human welfare. From 1978 to 2010, China created its second miracle, that is, while its per capita income increased rapidly, it realized major progress in education, health, and human development, significantly narrowing the relative gap

---

[19] Before 1949, China's death rate was 20 %; infant mortality rates were as high as 20 %; and mean life expectancy was approximately 35 years, at the 1820 level for Western Europe (36 years), lower than that of the United States in 1820 (39 years).

with the United States concerning such major indicators. In fact, China even succeeded to catch up. Between 2010 and 2030, China will create its third miracle in human welfare.

In terms of per capita income, no matter what computing method is used, the catch up coefficient in per capita GDP for China relative to the United States will increase from 10 to 25% in 2010 to 50% or higher by 2030. In terms of education, the catch up coefficient for average years of schooling in China relative to the United States will increase from 73.8 to 88.0% by 2030. In terms of health, the gap in mean life expectancy between China and the United States will narrow from 5 years in 2007 to 1.3 years by 2030, with the healthy life expectancy to narrow from 4 years to 0.3 years. In terms of HDI, the catch up coefficient for the HDI of China relative to the United States will increase from 74% in 2010 to 84% by 2030.

In terms of either economic wealth or human welfare, China will surpass the United States by 2030, when China's GDP aggregate will be when China's GDP aggregate will be 2.0–2.2 times that of the United States and its GHDI will be 3.23 times greater.

References

Barro RJ, Jong-Wha Lee (2010) A new data set of educational attainment in the world, 1950–2010, NBER Working Paper No. 15902. NBER, Cambridge

CIA (2010) The world factbook. CIA, Washington, DC

Deng Xiaoping (1993) To uphold socialism we must eliminate poverty April 26, 1987. In: Selected works of Deng Xiaoping, vol 3. People's Publishing House, Beijing, p 224

Hu Jintao (2007) Hold high the great banner of socialism with Chinese characteristics and strive for new victories in building a complete well-off society. Report to the 17th national congress of the communist party of China on Oct. 15, Beijing

Jiang Zemin (2005) Build a complete well-off society and opening up new ground in the cause of socialism with Chinese characteristic – Report to the 16th National Party Congress. In Selected important documents since the 16th National Party Congress, Part 1. Central Documentation Press, Beijing, p 14

Ma Kai (ed) (2006) Reader guide "The 11th Five-year Outline Program for National Economic and Social Development of the People's Republic of China". Beijing Science and Technology Publishing House, Beijing, 2006, p 517

Mao Zedong (1949) Bankruptcy of idealist conception of history. In: Selected works of Mao Zedong, vol 4. People's Publishing House, Beijing

Mao Zedong (1999) Speech at the enlarged central work conference, January 30, 1962. In: Collected works of Mao Zedong, vol 8. People's Publishing House, Beijing, p 302

McCraw TK (2006) Creating modern capitalism: how entrepreneurs, companies, and countries triumphed in three industrial revolutions, Chinese edn. Jiangsu People's Publishing House, Nanjing, p 576

Qiao Lei (2010) Are the American poor poor. Finance Weekly, 11 Oct

State Statistical Bureau (2010) Statistical abstract 2010. State Statistical Press, Beijing, p 105

UNDP (2003) Human development report 2003. Millennium development goals: a compact among nations to end human Poverty, Chinese edn. Beijing Finance and Economic Publishing House, Beijing, p 103

UNDP (2010) Human development report 2010

World Bank (2009) World development report 2009, Chinese edn. Tsinghua University Press, Beijing

Chapter 7
A Society with Shared Wealth

> *Socialism does not mean allowing a few people to grow rich while the overwhelming majority live in poverty. No, that's not socialism. The greatest superiority of socialism is that it enables all the people to prosper, and common prosperity is the essence of socialism (Deng Xiaoping 1993a).*

Deng Xiaoping (1990)

Since the beginning of human civilization, "equality for all and common prosperity" has been either the utopian dream of philosophers and poets or the grandiose rhetoric of politicians. However, the reality is quite different: "Behind the vermilion gates of the rich, meat and wine go to waste, but along the road are bones of the poor who have frozen to death" (a Chinese proverb). It has always been the case that "some families are joyful and some sad." There exists an insurmountable divide among mankind; this stems from family background, region, and social status, and it is true both now and in ancient times, in China and other countries.

Only after the socialist system was established was it possible for China to find, for the first time, a path to common prosperity. However, this path is so long that it often feels like a ten-thousand-mile journey. It is not only long but also complicated, with twists and turns, and it is challenging, exploratory, and innovative. In the era of Mao Zedong, China's population of millions stood up and achieved equality. The most important achievement of China's socialism is that it has created a society characterized by greater equality than any previous period in modern history. The people, especially the workers and peasants, have acquired the status of the masters of their own houses (Angang Hu 2008). The World Bank said in its China survey report at the beginning of the 1980s,

> China's past development strategy and the current system, in general, have created an extremely equal society. The city income inequality is extremely low. It may say there is no extreme poverty. But there is a gap in per capita income between cities and the countryside. The sufferings of the extremely poor population such as hunger, disease, high birth rate and

A. Hu et al., *China 2030*, DOI 10.1007/978-3-642-31328-8_7,

high infant mortality rate, widespread illiteracy and the fear of falling into dire poverty and
starvation that exist in other countries have been virtually eliminated. As a low-income
country, the mean life expectancy at birth is outstandingly high (67 years in 1980) (World
Bank Economic Study Tour 1983).

Thus, eliminating political inequality and social inequality is the first step toward
common prosperity.

The key objective and achievements of the reform and opening up was the elimination
of poverty, as poverty is not compatible with socialism. China had thus begun its
climb from a significant but poor power to a prosperous society. It adopted particular
development tactics to "allowing part of the areas and part of the people to get rich
first" (Deng Xiaoping 1993b) and thus succeeded in reducing the poverty levels of
the largest population in the world.

The notion of some regions and some people prospering earlier than others is not
a socialist ideal either. The architect of China's reform and opening up never
regarded that concept as the purpose of China's development; rather, it was made a
means to development within a given period. Deng Xiaoping commented, "China's
situation is very special. Even if 51% of the people get to prosper first, there are still
49 % or more than 600 million people still in poverty. There would be no stability.
There is no way that China can go toward capitalism. Only by building socialism
and realizing common prosperity, is it possible to have stability and development."[1]

Therefore, China had to start from scratch. It is certain that China will develop
from a prosperous society to one of common prosperity, realizing a historic step
forward.

In the next 20 years, China will enter an era of great harmony, characterized by
common development, common prosperity, and common wealth. Common development creates common prosperity and common prosperity leads to common wealth.
The purpose of both common development and common prosperity is to achieve
common wealth. Common wealth will narrow the gaps in the following three areas:
the rural/urban gap, regional gap, and the gap among individuals. These gaps lie not
only in income but also in terms of development, including the multi-dimensional
indicators of income, education, health, and public services. The realization of common
wealth means that both urban and rural residents, people living in either eastern
coastal regions or western inland provinces, and workers and peasants will live a
relatively wealthy life, receive high-quality public services, and share equitably in
the fruits of development.

In the next 20 years, there will be a great convergence of four key dimensions in
China: convergence at a regional economic development level, the convergence of
urban and rural incomes and standards of living, convergence of public services
among different regions, and convergence in HDI (measuring the level of social
development). All people will enjoy a high level of social security. There will also

---

[1] Speech by Deng Xiaoping in April 1990 when he met with Xie Guomin, Chairman of Chia Tai
Group of Thailand, from *Deng Xiaoping Chronicles (1975–1997)* Part II, p. 1312, Central
Documentation Press, 2004.

be convergence in per capita GDP, per capita revenue, and in urban and rural Engel's coefficient, which measures the level of social development, mean life expectancy at birth, average years of schooling, and HDI.

Common wealth is the basic orientation for socialist development—this is the desire of China's population. It is where their fundamental interests lie. They will reach political consensus and form synergy under the leadership of the Communist Party of China.

Common Wealth Shared by Both Urban and Rural Areas

The dual urban and rural structure is a particular feature of China. More than 180 years ago, China's traditional agrarian society disintegrated to give way to the current dual urban/rural structure. Since its creation more than 60 years ago, China's dual urban/rural structure has been continually reinforced, and over the last 30 years or so, the dual structure has grown to include triple and quadruple structures. The basic orientation for the following decades is sure to follow this unique historical logic and develop toward the integration of a quadruple structure. Urban/rural common prosperity will give way to urban/rural integration. The direct expression of the integration of multi-structures is the basic elimination of the rural population living in poverty and the convergence of income and standards of living for urban and rural areas.

China will seek a convergence in urban/rural income. As there are significant differences in the costs of living between cities and countryside, the urban/rural income gap calculated using the current price method appears higher than that using the constant price method. If calculated using constant price, the greatest urban/rural income gap occurred in 2009, with urban income 2.7 times greater than rural income. The current price method produced a rate showing urban income as 3.3 times greater. In 2010, for the first time in recent years, the speed of rural per capita net income growth exceeded that of the disposable income of urban residents. Thus, the income gap has been significantly narrowed. Between 2010 and 2030, rural income will grow more quickly than urban income, with the gap continuing to be narrowed. If calculated using the constant price method, the urban/rural income gap will reduce to a gap of 2.5 times by 2015, and then to 2.4 by 2020. The gap is expected to reduce further to 2.2 times by 2030, slightly lower than the disparity at the beginning of China's reform. By 2030, if calculated using the current price method, the disposable income of urban areas will reach approximately 90,000 yuan and the rural net income will be close to 40,000 yuan (see Fig. 7.1)

China will also seek the convergence of standards of living between urban and rural areas. As the regional costs between cities and rural areas are different, the most appropriate indicator to reflect the real urban/rural gap is the Engel's coefficient, which is obviously less than the urban/rural income gap. Since 1978, China's urban/rural Engel's coefficients have been steadily declining, with the gap continually narrowing. The urban Engel's coefficient will reduce to less than 40% by 2012,

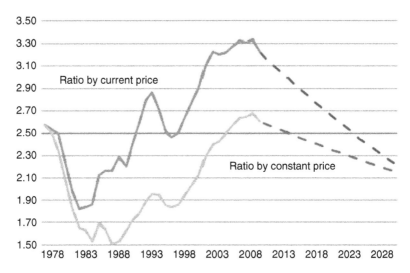

Fig. 7.1 Ratio of urban disposable income to rural Net income (1978–2030) (Note: *Upper curve* indicates urban/rural income ratio by current price and the lower curve represents urban/rural income ratio by constant price. Sources: Data for 1978–2010 are based on the "Collection of Statistical Materials of the 60 years of New China", China Statistical Abstract 2011; data for 2011–2030 are the estimates of the author)

with China's consumption structure transitioning from a prosperous to a wealthy structure. In addition, the living quality of urban and rural areas will be significantly improved (see Fig. 7.2).

In 2010, the gap in the Engel's coefficient between urban and rural areas was approximately 10 years, that is, the rural Engel's coefficient was at the level of urban areas in 2000. By 2020, this will be narrowed to 7 years and then to 3 years by 2030. In terms of consumption structure, urban expenditure on food, clothing, domestic electrical appliances, and other durable consumer goods will steadily decrease and expenditure on housing, medicine, education, culture, and entertainment will increase.

Many aspects of rural life, including agricultural production, the living conditions of peasants, rural development, and agricultural labor power transfer, are undergoing "modernization." Such agricultural modernization includes rural industrialization, peasants engaging in multiple occupations, and the urbanization of migrant workers. In addition, agriculture's role in the national economy is becoming smaller, enabling the non-agricultural population (representing more than 90% of the population) to support and strengthen agriculture. The urban population has already exceeded and will further exceed the rural population. Thus, urban areas will support and buoy the rural areas. Government revenue will also increase, making it possible to increase investments in agriculture, rural areas, and peasants, and to reduce the tax burdens of agriculture and peasants. These measures will help to narrow the urban/rural gap and to realize common prosperity for both urban and rural areas.

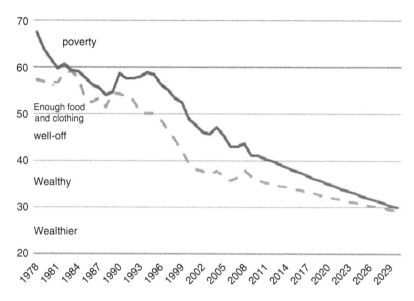

Fig. 7.2 Urban/rural Engel's coefficient (1978–2030) (Note: *The solid line* represents the urban Engel's coefficient and *broken line* represents the rural Engel's coefficient. Sources: "Collection of Statistical Materials of the 60 years of New China", China Statistical Abstract 2011; data for 2011–2030 are the estimates of the author)

Common Prosperity Among Different Regions

Regional development disparity has been a classic feature of China's national conditions (Angang Hu et al. 1995). "One China, four worlds" captures our national perspective and is a vividly accurate description of the regional gaps in development.[2] However, since the 1990s, regional disparities have been reduced as the per capita GDP gap narrowed. By 2010, the regional gap coefficient in per capita GDP dropped to its lowest level of 0.56 since the beginning of the reform and opening up, lower than the 1990s level of 0.60.

In the next 20 years, China will experience a general convergence of regional development. Since reform, China's regional gaps have been through four stages: development indicators converged in the 1980s; development indicators diverged in the 1990s; entering the twenty-first century, most indicators converged; and in the

---

[2] The first world refers to Shanghai and Beijing, which have attained a level higher than the average of upper-middle income countries; the second refers to Tianjin, Guangdong, Zhejiang, Jiangsu, Fujian, and Liaoning, which have attained a level higher than the lower-middle income countries but lower than upper-middle income countries; the third world refers to Hebei and central northeast China and north China, which have attained a level higher than the average of low-income countries but lower than lower-middle income countries. The fourth world refers to the poorer areas of the central and western areas of the country, areas inhabited by national minorities, rural areas, and remote regions that have levels lower than the average of low-income countries (Angang Hu 2001).

following 20 years all indicators will converge, with the gaps becoming narrower. By 2030, the urban/rural gaps in public service and HDI, and those among regions, will become the smallest ever. This situation will essentially realize the uniformity of HDI and the equalization of basic public services among different regions, between rural and urban areas, and among China's various population groups. The gap in the standard of living between urban and rural residents and among various population groups will be greater than the gap in public services, but not a significant gap. The gap in urban/rural income and regional economic development levels will be greater than the rural/urban standards of living and various population groups, but compared with the current state, it will drop significantly (see Table 7.1). Public policies will become better able to regulate China's multi-dimensional gaps, as will their processes and strengths. Thus, a public service system and a high-level social security system, for both the urban and rural populations, will begin to take shape.

We predict that the regional per capita GDP gap coefficient will continue to fall, to 0.40 by 2020 and 0.37 by 2030 (see Fig. 7.3). By 2030, China's regional disparity in per capita GDP will be closer to the regional disparity of the United States as at 2000.[3] If Beijing, Tianjin, and Shanghai are not included, the real disparity coefficient will be much lower. Although regional economic development disparity cannot be entirely eliminated, it will be maintained at a very low level.

With the common development of all regions and China's constant convergence, the original "four worlds" will gradually become "three worlds" (as is currently occurring), then "two worlds", and ultimately "one China, one world." By 2030, China will be close to realizing its desired high-income levels, with approximately half of the provinces and autonomous regions having reached the high-income level and the remainder will have attained the level of upper-middle income countries. By 2030, the per capita GDP of six of China's provinces, municipalities, and autonomous regions will get closer to that of the United States and the other seven will overtake the United States. As of 2010, no province had attained the current per capita GDP level of the United States. However, by 2020, Shanghai, Beijing, and Tianjin will have overtaken the United States. By 2030, Jiangsu, Zhejiang, Guangdong, and Inner Mongolia may also have overtaken the United States in this regard.

The narrowing of regional disparities is a natural trend of economic development. The investment model in the central and western parts of China is similar to that in the eastern coastal areas. A model characterized by greater optimized investments will be introduced soon. Investment in human capital and ecological resources will become the major drive for central and western China to narrow the disparities with eastern coastal areas. The disparities in regional development will reduce because of an adjustment in industrial distribution, which has been motivated by government policies, changes in population, and economic geography. Such policies include the West Development Strategy (1999), the strategy of invigorating the older industrial regions such as northeast China (2004) and the Central Area Increase Strategy

---

[3] The per capital GDP gap coefficient among the 50 states of the United States in 2000 was 0.32 (see Kessler and Lessmann 2009).

Table 7.1 Disparity coefficient of major development indicators of various provinces and autonomous regions (1980–2030)

	1980	1990	2000	2010	2015	2020	2030
Per capita GDP	0.90	0.60	0.70	0.56	0.46	0.40	0.37
Per capita revenue	2.04	1.11	1.05	1.09	1.03	1.05	1.00
Per capita expenditure	0.91	0.61	0.76	0.60	0.45	0.35	0.25
Engel's coefficient							
Urban	0.15	0.12	0.10	0.11	0.10	0.10	0.09
Rural	0.16	0.15	0.16	0.14	0.13	0.12	0.10
Mean life expectancy	0.22	0.18	0.13	0.10	0.09	0.08	0.07
Ave. years of school	0.25	0.20	0.16	0.12	0.11	0.10	0.09
HDI	0.25	0.16	0.10	0.09	0.08	0.08	0.07

Sources: "Collection of Statistical Materials of the 60 Years of New China," China Statistical Yearbook (1981), China Statistical Abstract (2011); data for 2020 and 2030 are the estimates of the author

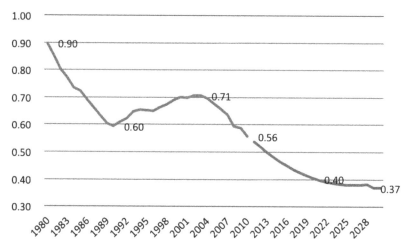

Fig. 7.3 Disparity coefficients in per capita GDP of various regions (1980–2030) (Note: Data for 1980–2010 were calculated using the constant price method. Sources: "Collection of Statistical Materials of the 60 years of New China", China Statistical Abstract 2011; data for 2011–2030 are the estimates of the author)

(2006) and the transfer of payments, equalization of basic public services, large-scale infrastructure construction, ecology-building and ecological security screens under the framework of regional integration.

China has the world's highest population, and was once the poorest nation. Over the past 60 years, especially in the 30 years or so since the reform and opening up, China has created the biggest miracle in the history of human development. This miracle is not only represented by the amazing speed of economic development but also in the significant progress in human development. As seen from a regional level, China's various provinces and autonomous regions have achieved a high level of human development and the trend of convergence has arrived.

China will enter the stage of high human development by 2030. According to the latest UNDP calculation method for HDI, China's HDI in 2010 was 0.663, representing mid-level development. However, some areas, such as Shanghai, Beijing, Tianjin, Liaoning, Zhejiang, Jiangsu, Guangdong, Jilin, Shandong, and Inner Mongolia, have already attained high human development levels. China as a whole is likely to bring its HDI above 0.700 by 2015 to reach a high development level. By 2020, the majority of provinces will be categorized as having a high human development level. Some developed coastal provinces will attain an extremely high level in human development. By 2030, the human development levels of all regions will have increased (see Table 7.2). In 2030, China will rank in 40th in the world's HDI.

If we further divide China's provinces according to human development levels, in 1980, 97.15 % of China's population was at the low level and 2.85 % were at the middle level. By 2000, 8.84 % of the population was at the low level, 88.7 % were at the middle level, and 1.42 % of the population was at the high level. As of 2010, 63.63 % of the population was at the middle level and 36.37 % at the high level. By 2030, approximately 90 % of the population will be at the high level, with Beijing, Shanghai, Tianjin, Liaoning, Zhejiang, Jiangsu, Guangdong, Jilin, and Inner Mongolia at the extremely high level (with a combined population of 29.18 %). Only Yunnan, Guizhou, and Tibet will be at the middle level (with their combined population of 6.28 %). Simultaneously, because of the convergence of regional economic development levels, education and health levels will also converge, with the gap coefficient in HDI reducing from 0.25 in 1980, to 0.09 by 2010, and 0.07 by 2030.

Equalization of Basic Public Services

The goal of development is to enable people to have the ability to live a better life. This means an investment in their education, health, and their abilities for risk management (World Bank 2006). The overall development depends on economic development levels and on the degree of equalization regarding the supply of basic public services. In China's new era and stage of development, the equalization of basic public services has become a major strategic task of scientific and harmonious development, and the basic responsibility of government at all levels. The provision of a basic public service is the most fundamental of public services. It is closely associated with the true and immediate interests of the people, and their key concerns. The equalization of basic public service means to enable all people to enjoy the same rights and a similar level of basic public services. The realization of such equalization represents the basic function and responsibility of modern government. It must ensure that all members of society, whether they are urban or rural residents living in developed or poor areas, and irrespective of their social status, should all be able to enjoy similar levels of public services, including education, public health and basic medical care, basic social security, public employment service, and a basic housing guarantee. The government must set up a basic public

Table 7.2 City groupings and regional changes in HDI (1980–2030)

	Low HD level	Middle HD level	High HD level	Extremely high HD level
1980	Liaoning, Guangdong, Jiangsu Heilongjiang, Zhejiang, Jilin, Shandong, Shanxi, Fujian, Hainan, Hebei, Hubei, Inner Mongolia, Xinjiang, Hunan, Shaanxi, Henan, Ningxia, Guangxi, Sichuan, Jiangxi, Anhui, Chongqing, Qinghai, Gansu, Yunnan, Guizhou, and Tibet	Shanghai, Beijing, and Tianjin		
2000	Qinghai, Gansu, Yunnan, Guizhou, and Tibet	Tianjin, Liaoning, Guangdong, Zhejiang, Jiangsu, Heilongjiang, Fujian, Shandong, Jilin, Hebei, Hainan, Hubei, Inner Mongolia, Shanxi, Xinjiang, Chongqing, Henan, Hunan, Shanxi, Guangxi, Jiangxi, Sichuan, Ningxia, and Anhui	Shanghai and Beijing	
2010		Hebei, Heilongjiang, Fujian, Shanxi, Chongqing, Hubei, Shaanxi, Henan, Hunan, Hainan, Xinjiang, Ningxia, Guangxi, Jiangxi, Anhui, Sichuan, Qinghai, Gansu, Yunnan, Guizhou, and Tibet	Shanghai, Beijing, Tianjin, Liaoning, Zhejiang, Jiangsu, Guangdong, Jilin, Shandong, and Inner Mongolia	

(continued)

Table 7.2 (continued)

	Low HD level	Middle HD level	High HD level	Extremely high HD level
2020		Qinghai, Gansu, Yunnan, Guizhou, and Tibet	Liaoning, Zhejiang, Jiangsu, Guangdong, Jilin, Shandong, Inner Mongolia, Hebei, Heilongjiang, Fujian, Shaanxi, Chongqing, Hubei, Shaanxi, Henan, Hunan, Hainan, Xinjiang, Ningxia, Guangxi, Jiangxi, Anhui, and Sichuan	Shanghai, Beijing, and Tianjin
2030		Yunnan, Guizhou, and Tibet	Heilongjiang, Chongqing, Shandong, Hubei, Hunan, Ningxia, Shanxi, Shaanxi, Xinjiang, Hebei, Henan, Fujian, Guangxi, Hainan, Jiangxi, Anhui, Sichuan, Qinghai, and Gansu	Beijing, Shanghai, Tianjin, Liaoning, Jiangsu, Guangdong, Zhejiang, Jilin, and Inner Mongolia

Note: The provinces are grouped in order from highest to lowest HDI; data are calculated by the author based on the new UNDP method; for HDI data for various regions, see Appendix Table 2

Sources: UNDP, Human Development Report (2010) and Human Development Database; China Human Development Report (2010); national population censuses; Education Ministry's Education Statistics Bulletin of corresponding years; data for 2020–2030 are the estimates of the author

service system best suited to the national conditions, which should be comprehensive, cover both rural and urban areas, and is sustainable so as to gradually narrow the gaps in standards of living and public services between rural and urban areas. At its core is the equalization of opportunities and outcomes, however, differences still exist (Zhang Ping 2011).

The quality and level of basic public services mutually supplement and reinforce each other. In the next 20 years, the basic public service system will develop from a low-level broad ranging system to a high-quality and homogeneous structure. Although there are disparities in economic development levels and income levels between rural and urban areas, and among different regions, there will be a convergence of basic public services, especially with regard to output indicators, in these areas. In addition, the equalization of basic public services has transitioned from urban and rural areas and regions to various population groups, realizing the objective of these services for all of China's people, with the level and quality of public services to be the same for all rural/urban areas and regions.

The various existing disparities between urban/rural basic public service levels are moving toward convergence. In terms of health levels for urban and rural areas, the convergence is obvious. The urban/rural difference in mean life expectancy reduced from 5 years in 1990 to 2.6 years in 2010. The difference in infant mortality rates reduced from 41 deaths per thousand births in 1990 to 7.3 per thousand by 2010, and the rates are likely to be the same by 2030. The difference in the death rate of rural and urban children under 5 years of age was 40 deaths per thousand in 1990 and reduced to 9 per thousand by 2010, and the rates are likely to be the same by 2030. The urban/rural difference in pregnancy and maternal deaths was nearly 80 per thousand in 1990 and in 2010. The number of deaths per 100,000 pregnant and maternal women was 15 and it is expected to be the same in 2030 (see Table 7.3)

China will essentially eliminate rural poverty. China was a large but poor power; in 1981, 490 million people each spent less than one dollar a day, with China's total poor population accounting for 35% of the world's total. According to China's official poverty line, the poverty occurrence rate has dropped from 18.5% in 1981 to 2.0% in 2010. The number of rural poor has reduced from 152 million to 26.88 million.[4] The World Bank commented that a decline in the number of poor of this magnitude over such a short period is without precedent (World Bank 2009). During this period, the number of poor in all developing countries declined from 1.5 billion to 1.1 billion. In other words, without China's efforts, the number of poor in developing countries would have risen instead of declined in the last 20 years of the twentieth century.

Based on the rate of rural income growth, China is likely to eliminate rural poverty by approximately 2020. Although a low-income group will still exist, extreme poverty will no longer exist. To alleviate rural poverty a rural minimum income

---

[4] China's rural poverty standard is adjusted annually. It was 100 yuan/year in 1978, 300 yuan/year in 1990, and 625 yuan/year in 2000. The current standard for a poor county is 1,196 yuan/year (used since 2009).

Table 7.3 Major urban/rural health indicators (1990–2030)

	1990	2000	2010	2015	2020	2030
Mean life expectancy (years)						
Urban	72.0		74.8a			
Rural	67.4		72.2a			
Infant mortality rate (%)						
Urban	17.3	11.8	5.8	6	5	4
Rural	58.0	37.0	16.1	14	10	5
Death rate of children under 5 (%)						
Urban	20.9	13.8	7.3	7	5	4
Rural	71.1	45.7	20.1	15	10	5
Death rate of pregnant and maternal women (1/100,000)						
Urban	45.9	29.3	29.7	15	10	7
Rural	112.5	69.6	30.1	30	18	10

Note: 'a' indicates data for 2005
Source: Data for 1990–2010 were sourced from the website of the Ministry of Public Health; data for 2015 and 2020 were sourced from a project group of the Ministry of Public Health: "Healthy China 2020 Research Report", May 2010; data for 2030 are the estimates of the author

insurance will be introduced (similar to urban areas). If calculated using a poverty line of 1.25 dollars a day, the rural poverty occurrence rate was 90% in 1978. However, this reduced to 60.2% by 1990 and 7.9% in 2010. By 2015, it will be less than 1%. Thus, extreme poverty will be essentially eliminated by 2020 (see Table 7.4).

There will also be a convergence of inter-regional basic public service levels. The high/low disparities of mean life expectancy among regions have reduced from 16.9 years in 1980 to 13.7 years in 2010, and will further decline to 9.1 years by 2030. Correspondingly, the disparity coefficient of mean life expectancy among regions reduced from 0.067 in 1980 to 0.043 in 2010, and will be at 0.035 by 2030. The high/low disparities of average years of schooling among regions reduced from 5.6 years in 1980 to 5.3 years in 2010, and will then reduce to 4.8 years. The corresponding disparity coefficient in this area reduced from 0.249 in 1980 to 0.119 in 2010, and will decrease to 0.089 by 2030. The regional disparities in average years of schooling and mean life expectancy, the basic measure of basic education and public health service outcomes are lower than the per capita GDP disparities in terms of both the general measurement and the reduction of GDP disparities.

Rural/urban and regional boundaries in terms of basic public services will gradually be abolished and equalization will be realized for all people. With the current economic and social development, China's population structure is undergoing profound changes. The traditional urban/rural dual structure will gradually give way to a quadruple structure with a fusion of traditional agriculture, rural industry, urban regular economy, and an urban irregular economy. This will result in four major population groups: peasants, migrant workers in rural areas, migrant workers in urban areas, and urban residents. As seen from the perspective of these groups, basic public services have not yet been equalized, as urban residents enjoy more

Table 7.4 Poverty occurrence rates for China (1978–2020)

Year	Poverty occurrence rate under intl. poverty line (1.25 dollar/day) (%)	China's rural poverty line (yuan/year)	Poverty occurrence rate under China's rural poverty line (%)
1978	90.0	100	30.7
1985	69.4	206	14.8
1990	60.2	200	9.4
1995	54.1	530	7.1
2000	35.6	625	3.5
2005	15.9	683	2.5
2010	7.9	1,274	2.8
2015	1.0	2,000	1.0
2020	0.1	3,000	0.1

Sources: Data for China's rural poverty in 1978–2010 was sourced from State Statistical Bureau (2011); data on poverty according to international poverty line were sourced from the World Bank, World Development Indicator 2010; data for 2010, 2015, and 2020 are the estimates of the author

and better public services than the other three groups. However, the public service system is in the progress of being improved and current policies are also oriented toward improving these services, aiming at full coverage and high supply level. By 2030, services will be equalized among the four population groups. With regard to social security, a high-level unified structure will be realized. In terms of public services, the four major population groups will enjoy similar primary medical services. With regard to education services, the four major groups will have uniform access to China's compulsory primary education, senior secondary school education will be largely available to all, and university enrolment rates will increase. In terms of employment services, the four groups will be able to enjoy a basic employment service. Migrant workers from rural areas will have access to a better service regarding urban job opportunities.

A basic public service system that covers both rural and urban areas, equalized among different regions and population groups, embodies the "visible hand of government" and is where the essence of livelihood-oriented scientific development lies. It is also an important manifestation of all people sharing the fruits of reform and development. It is, first of all, necessary to realize the convergence of the basic public services in rural and urban areas and among different regions. Then the government will commit more resources to central and western areas where public services have a weak foundation. Thus, the supply level and quality will be increased. The next step will be to realize convergence among different population groups and gradually break down the boundaries between urban and rural areas and among different regions, providing uniform and seamless basic public services.

China's social security system will transition from the full coverage of urban and rural areas and regions, to the full coverage of various population groups. At present, many forms of social insurance and social relief systems have been established in regular employment departments in cities and town. Urban non-regular employment, rural non-agricultural departments and rural traditional agricultural areas have low coverage and low insurance levels. In some areas, various pilot projects have been launched, but they do enjoy wide spread application. As part of China's basic public services, the development and fine-tuning of the social security system also follows the gradual transition from urban/rural and regional integration to the integration of all population groups. The main social security and social relief elements will break the traditional urban/rural and regional boundaries according to the four population groups and realize full population uniformity and seamless coverage so as to achieve the goal that all people, irrespective of urban or rural residence and workplace, can enjoy the same level of insurance and can freely transfer the basic social security services. We hold that this goal will be realized by 2030.

The aim of a basic social security system is to increase the capabilities of the people to withstand various risks and effectively increase their income levels. The first and foremost task of any country in the process of developing toward a high-income stage is to establish a social security system. In addition, the building of a social security system is an area of public service that involves the greatest difficulties, problems, and pressures. China's social security system has been developed from scratch, established after the reform and opening up. Great progress has been achieved within a short timeframe. China has essentially established a comprehensive social security system, with a variety of social insurance and social relief policies covering increasingly greater areas and accompanied by greater levels of insurance. With the strong political will of the government and its leaders (and when it has enough public resources), China is likely to build the world's largest and highest level social security system by 2030. At that time, China's population will be covered and everyone will enjoy a high level of social security.

Summary: Toward a Common Wealth Society

In reviewing the development paths of other countries, a social phenomenon of the widening of urban/rural and regional disparities appears as a difficult trend to avoid in the process of economic and social development. Only a few countries have successfully coped with such disparities to become successful models with both high income and high disparities. However, most countries have long fallen in the mire of excessively large social disparities, thus leading to incessant social conflicts, economic stagnation, and the middle-income trap. The narrowing of disparities and the realization of common prosperity and common wealth is a difficult subject of study in developmental economics, especially for a large country like China, and successfully holding in check widening developmental disparities will entail extremely high governance costs.

According to our analysis and prediction, China's urban/rural development disparities and regional development gap will converge between 2010 and 2030; public services will be equalized and everyone will enjoy a relatively high level of social security. However, what are the required favorable conditions that will enable China to break the development paradox and go beyond the middle-income trap to realize common prosperity?

These include:

1. **Strong political will of leaders.** They should regard the narrowing of social development disparities as the core of its scientific development and make the underdeveloped rural areas, the central and western areas, and the urban migrant workers the focus of all policies. Our political leaders will then need to encourage the poorer populations and areas to increase their income and narrow the development disparities from many directions.
2. **Adhere to the socialist road.** It is necessary to regard common prosperity as the focal point of all development policies. Especially on entering the twenty-first century, the elimination of development disparities has become the number one starting point from which to formulate economic and social policies. In addition, the superiority of socialism has been showcased as its ability to amass many resources to achieve something substantial has been called into play. As a result, a large number of policies have been produced aimed at eliminating the disparities between city and countryside, among different regions, and different population groups.
3. **Committing substantial state revenue to support efforts to narrow development disparities.** In 1994, after the revenue sharing system was introduced, central and local governments greatly enhanced their financial resources. In 2010, the financial resources available from the five government public financial resources, such as integrated public fiscal budget, government fund budget, social security budget, state capital operation gain budget, and extra-budgetary funds reached 15.6 trillion yuan, 34.1% of GDP. In the next 20 years, China will still be at a prosperous level, a crucial period for building a common wealth society. It will be an important strategic opportunity period, which will provide solid and effective support to demand, finance, and institutions to encourage the equalization of basic public services.
4. **Local innovations will provide valuable experience.** How can we realize common prosperity? The answer can be found in local innovations. That is, we have seen the practice of the methodology for creating common prosperity. For instance, Chongqing Municipality has addressed the problem of narrowing three disparities, for example, lowering the Gini coefficient, narrowing the urban/rural gap, and narrowing the "one circle" and "two wings" disparities. All these indicators have been advanced nationwide and are of great demonstrative significance (see Box 7.1). Chongqing has its own distinct features in its practice of achieving common prosperity. It may be summarized as a "two-pronged attack." The first is to make the cake larger, that is, significantly develop the economy and let its people create wealth; the second is to cut and distribute the cake, that is, to actively adjust the production relationship and distribution relationship. When we look back after ten years or even after 20 years, the historical significance should be revealed. Chongqing can offer its experiences to the whole nation and even some lessons. Either way, as experience or lessons, Chongqing will also represent the wealth of the nation.

Box 7.1 Chongqing's Exploration into Common Prosperity (2011)

Chongqing is typical of development disparity, with wide regional disparities, urban and rural gaps, and disparities among population groups. Its "two wings" have 14 state-level poor counties and 1,600 poor villages. Large city and rural areas co-exist. The urban/rural income gap is 3.3:1. Chongqing's Gigi coefficient is 0.42. The urban and rural populations covered by minimum cost of living insurance have reached 1.7 million.'

In July 2011, the Chongqing Municipal Party Committee decided at its 9th plenary session of the provincial congress to recognize the importance of the narrowing of the disparities in three major areas. It was seen as an important breakthrough in implementing scientific development and accelerating change in the economic development model to embark on the road to improve livelihoods and achieve common prosperity.

The municipality will now strive to narrow the disparities between urban and rural areas, among different districts, and between the poor and the rich. By 2015, it will synchronize the growth of total economic aggregate and income, reduce income disparity to 2.51, the development disparities of "the circle and two wings" to approximately 21, and the Gini coefficient to 0.35. It will promote the equalization of public services and realize basic social security for all.

It has come out with a 12-point measure to realize full employment, encourage innovative undertakings to create wealth, increase peasants' incomes, especially income from property, increase the percentage of income in GDP, display the regulatory rules of state-owned enterprises to encourage the equalization of basic public services, and support the development of districts and counties, and to launch developmental poverty relief projects.

The exploration and experience of Chongqing has nationwide significance. It will serve as a model to emulate for common prosperity with distinctly Chinese characteristics.

Source: http://www.cq.gov.cn

References

Angang Hu (ed) (Feb 2001) Regions and development: New Western Development Strategy. China Planning Press, Beijing

Angang Hu (2008) On China's political economics (1949–1976), 3rd edn. Tsinghua University Press, Beijing, p 534

Angang Hu, Wang Shaoguang, Kang Xiaoguang (Jan 1995) Report on China's regional disparities. Liaoning People's Publishing House, Shenyyang

Kessler AS, Lessmann C (Mar 2009) Interregional redistribution and regional disparities: how equalization does (not) work

Deng Xiaoping (1993a) Seize the opportunity to develop the economy, December 24 1990. In: Selected works of Deng Xiaoping, vol III. People's Publishing House, Beijing, p 364

Deng Xiaoping (1993b) There is No fundamental contradiction between socialism and a market economy October 23, 1985. In: Selected works of Deng Xiaoping, vol III. People's Publishing House, Beijing, p 149

State Statistical Bureau (2011) China Statistical Abstract 2011.China Statistical Press, Beijing, p 106

World Bank (Feb 2006) World development 2006: equity and development. Tsinghua University Press, Beijing, p 132

World Bank Economic Study Tour (1983) China: development of socialist economy, Chinese edn. China Finance and Economics Press, Beijing

Zhang Ping (ed) (Apr 2011) Reader guide, "12th Five-year Program for national economic and social development of the People's Republic of China". People's Publishing House, Beijing, p 336

World Bank (Mar 2009) From poor areas to poor people: China's evolving poverty reduction agenda. An assessment of poverty and inequality in China

Chapter 8
Green China

Harmony between man and nature.

Chinese classical philosophy

The concept of "harmony between man and nature" embodies both the respect of nature and being close to nature—this is the highest pursuit of Chinese philosophy. Such philosophies are captured in the following verses,

Two orioles are singing in the green willow tree; egrets are flying in the blue sky in a neat line

The Sun rises out of the sparkling water, fiery red; the spring water is clear and blue when spring sets in Green trees surround the village; outside the Castle are green peaks.[1]

These popular verses depict the blue skies, crystal clear water, and green mountains of the beautiful homeland of the Chinese people, living in perfect harmony with nature.

However, China's agricultural past, lasting thousands of years, has inevitably overtaxed its ecological assets. Before 1949, China's ecology was already vulnerable, with the levels of forestation and the total volume of standing stock reaching historical lows. Since entering an age of modern economy, China's industrialization and urbanization have exacerbated the ecological damage via the excessive consumption of energy and resources, accompanied by large-scale pollution. Even as recently as the late 1990s, China faced an ecological crisis on a scale never seen before, accompanied by a significant ecological deficit.[2]

---

[1] These lines are quoted from Du Fu's "Five-character verse", Bai Juyi's "In Memory of South China" and Meng Haoran's "Passing by the Village of an Old Friend".

[2] The authors' basic evaluation of China's ecological environment at that time is as follows: preexisting problems; negative impacts of modern development, lack of proper care; degradation and pollution, with local improvements but deterioration as a whole; governance capacity falls far short of the speed of destruction; and the environmental quality has been deteriorating, resulting in large-scale ecological destruction and environmental pollution, broadest in coverage and the most serious in Chinese history (Hu Angang et al. 1990).

From a global perspective, China has become a superpower in terms of energy consumption, greenhouse gas emissions, and pollutant discharge. At present, China consumes 20.3% of the world's energy and 48.2% of the world's coal, making it the biggest consumer of this particular natural resource in the world.[3] Furthermore, China discharges 20% of the world's carbon dioxide emissions, as well as methane (15.1%), and nitrogen chloride (15.0%), and is therefore the world's biggest emissions producer.[4] China also emits 32.9% of the world's sulfur dioxide emissions, nitrogen oxides (20.7%) and various particles (33.5%), ranking first in the world for such emissions.

China's ecological environment is facing serious challenges. Desertification affects 27.3% of China's land mass and nearly four million people; water loss and soil erosion have reached levels of 38%, with the loss of soil reaching five billion tons. These conditions pose serious threats to the diversity of China's ecosystem, species, and gene pools, with 20–40% of its biological species under threat (The Ecology and Environment Strategy Study Group of the Chinese Academy of Sciences 2009).

In the mid-1990s, China designed its first sustainable development strategy[5] to address its ecological and environmental challenges. During the 11th five-year plan period, a local ecological surplus began to appear and forested areas increased, the discharge of major pollutants reduced, and China's environmental quality improved.[6] How will China realize sustainable development under the constraint of resources, energy, environment, and climate change in the next 20 years? Furthermore, what of green development? How will China turn a local ecological surplus into a nationwide ecological surplus? How should China realize green modernization and make green contributions to the world?

In the next 20 years, China will build on its local ecological surpluses to achieve a nationwide surplus. This development will arrest China's extensive history of

---

[3] See United Kingdom Petroleum (BP): World energy statistics 2010.

[4] Energy data was sourced from IEA, 2010; other data was sourced from the World Bank (World Bank 2008).

[5] On July 4, 1994, the State Council ratified the "White Paper on China's Populations, Environments and Development in the 21st Century". On September 28, 1995, the 5th plenary session of the 14th Central Committee of the Communist Party of China passed the "Proposals on the 9th five-year plan and the goals for the Year 2010", which officially put forward the sustainable development strategies. The document clearly calls for efforts to basically arrest environmental pollution and the deterioration of the ecology by the end of this century (20th) and to improve the environmental quality in some cities and areas, improve ecological deterioration, and the urban and rural environment by 2010.

[6] According to data provided by the Ministry of Environmental Protection, the controlled surface water of seven major waterways was better than third-class water, with the proportion rising from 41% in 2005 to 57%. The annual average concentration of sulfur dioxide in the air of urban areas dropped by 17% as compared with 2005. The number of cities above the prefectural level that reached or exceeded the second-class air quality standard rose to 79.6%. The proportion of thermal power desulphurization rose from 12% in 2005 to 80%; the sewage treatment rate rose from 52% in 2005 to 75%. Website of the Ministry of Environmental Protection.

ecological deterioration. This will manifest itself in the following ways: first, China's ecology will be markedly improved when its total coal consumption reaches its peak, delinking from economic growth; second, water resources will be brought under effective protection and water consumption will be further delinked with economic growth; third, the growth rate of carbon dioxide emissions will fall, with emission volumes delinking from economic growth; fourth, cultivated areas will essentially remain intact, with the red line (critical mark) for 120 million hectares of land under a strong level of protection; fifth, areas of ecological degradation area will reduce, including soil erosion and water loss areas, desertification, rocky desertification areas, and areas of damaged vegetation; sixth, an all-round improvement of environmental quality will be achieved, with China's skies turning blue once again, and clean waters and green mountains.

A Superpower of Forest Surpluses and Carbon Sink[7]

Scientists often describe forests as the lungs of the Earth. Without forests, the Earth cannot breathe properly. Forests absorb carbon dioxide and release oxygen, adsorb dust and purify both the air and water, help to conserve water, provide moisture to the soil, increase humidity, regulate the climate, offer shelter from wind, and reduce erosion and noise. China, as a vast country covering 9.60 million square kilometers with a population of more than one billion, is extremely deficient in terms of "lung capacity." Its per capita forest resource is only 20% of the world's average. China has very little capital in terms of forests, and its forestry products are low-ranking in terms of eco-product. In addition, the forest service is the rarest ecological service.

History shows a U-curve change in China's forest resources. Between 2069 BC and 221 BC, 46–60% of the land in China was covered in forest. However, China's agricultural civilization, which relied on the mercy of nature, reduced the forest cover to just 8.6% by 1948. Since the founding of the New China, China's forestry industry has exploited nature and the volume of standing stocks have reduced steadily (however, the industry has also planted many trees). Forested areas and the volume of standing stocks did not begin to increase until after the mid-1980s, when the government introduced its first forestry policies in 1998. Since then, a historic change has occurred, realizing the transition from timber-oriented production to ecological construction. This has essentially reversed the historical trend of the consistent reduction of forestry assets, resulting in an ecological surplus. While most other developing countries still survive on the achievements of their ancestors, China has taken the lead and has "planted trees to benefit the future generations." According to the latest assessment by the UN's FAO on global forest resources,

---

[7] This section is written with reference to the Study of New Green Policy and Forest Development Transition by the China Study Center of Tsinghua University entrusted to the State Forest Bureau, (project leader: Hu Angang; operators: Hu Angang and Liu Min), January 6, 2011.

forested areas worldwide are reducing by approximately 6,666,666 hectares annually, but in China, forested areas are increasing annually by 4,000,000 hectares (representing 53.2% of the world's total). Thus, forest cover has increased by approximately 7.86 percentage points since the founding of the New China; forested areas have grown by approximately 62% and the volume of standing stocks has increased by approximately 27%.

China has identified the acceleration of forestry construction as a national strategy and over the next 20 years China will become the world's fastest-growing state in terms of forest resources. The gap between China and other forestry superpowers will narrow at an accelerated speed. According to the national 12th five-year plan, by 2015, forest cover in China will reach 21.66% and forest standing stock will reach 14.3 billion cubic meters. According to the national outlined program on the utilization and protection of wooded land (2010–2020 years),[8] forest stock will reach 223 million hectares, 40 million hectares more than in 2005, forest coverage will exceed 23 %, and the volume of standing stock will reach 15.0 billion cubic meters by 2020. If this development trend continues, China's forest cover will reach 25 %, forest standing stock volumes 16 billion cubic meters, and forest areas 240 million hectares by 2030. Thus, China will rank fourth in the world (behind Russia, Brazil, and the United States) in terms of forest resources. Its gap with the United States will be reduced from 100 million hectares to 60 million hectares.

China's forests have become the world's largest artificial forest carbon sinks.[9] Between 2003 and 2008, China's standing forest stock registered a net increase of 1.123 billion cubic meters, averaging an annual net increase of 225 million cubic meters.[10] This is the equivalent to the average annual carbon sink of 410 million tons, 20.6 billion tons over a five-year period. By 2015, China's accumulated carbon sink will reach 26.1 billion tons and up to 29.28 billion ton by 2030 (representing an increase of 4.17 billion tons since 2010). China has become the world's largest artificial forest carbon sink, which is equivalent to a reduction of 4.17 billion tons of emissions.

In addition, China's forests have also become China's largest "reservoir." According to information provided by the State Forestry Administration, the water conserved in China's forests is equivalent to 80% of the total reservoir storage capacity, creating China's largest "reservoirs." The fresh water conserved in the wetlands in China accounts for 96% of total fresh water, which is China's largest

---

[8] It was adopted in principle at the State Council Executive Meeting on June 9, 2010.

[9] In the United Nations Framework Convention on Climate Change, "sink" means any process, activity, or mechanism that removes a greenhouse gas, aerosol, or a precursor of a greenhouse gas from the atmosphere. "Source" means any process or activity that releases a greenhouse gas, an aerosol or a precursor of a greenhouse gas into the atmosphere. A forest carbon sink is where the forest ecosystem absorbs carbon dioxide in the air and fixes it in vegetation or soil, thus reducing the carbon dioxide densification process, activity, or mechanism. Scientific studies show that every one cubic meter of standing stock can absorb 2.83 tons of carbon dioxide and release an average 1.62 tons of oxygen.

[10] 7th Nationwide Forest Inventory results.

"water source." With the expansion of forested areas and increase in forest stock volumes, China's forests will play a greater ecological role in the conservation of water, the prevention of soil erosion, and water loss.

China's forestry will also significantly contribute to an increase in employment levels. A study by the Beijing Forestry University showed that China's forestry industry employed 45.792 million people in 2008 and its associated industries may create .5–1.2 million jobs a year, representing a 10% increase in labor power. With the current economic development and the increase in forested areas, many new jobs will be created by the forestry industry (Table 8.1).

A Country of Harmony Between Its People and Water[11]

"Water is the kidney of the Earth," the "source of life," "a factor of production," and "the foundation of ecology." Water sources and the ecosystem are the most important of all ecological assets, and water conservancy facilities are the most important public assets. Such facilities represent public welfare and are important in terms of strategy and security.

"Building water conservancy projects to ward off floods has always been a matter of major importance for governing the country and pacifying the neighbors" (Hu Jintao 2011). Water resource development concerns not only flood control, water supply security, food security, but also economic, ecological, and state security.[12] The fundamental task of water conservancy development is to continually meet the needs of economic and social development.

Since the founding of the New China, China's water conservancy development in general has gone through three stages. 1949–1977 was a period of large-scale water conservancy construction, which focused on the construction of flood control and irrigation infrastructure to meet the needs of disaster prevention and food security. The second period, 1988–1997, represented a significant lag in water development. Due to investment deficiencies in water conservancy, funds for water conservancy construction were woefully inadequate. Supply and demand came into conflict with water security and ecological environment, and the gap continued to widen. The final stage, 1998–2010, was a transitional one. Because of the adverse effects of the severe floods in 1998, the state was forced to address the rapidly worsening water crisis. This heralded the first wave of water conservancy construction since the reform and opening up. However, it still fell short of the needs of economic and social development.

---

[11] This section refers to the China Study Center of Tsinghua University (project leaders: Hu Angang and Wang Yahua; operators: Wang Yahua and Hu Angang), "Study of water conservancy development stages-division, evaluation and strategic orientation", March 2010.

[12] Central No. 1 document, 2011.

Table 8.1 Changes in forest resources and carbon sink in China (1948–2050)

Year	Forest cover (%)	National forest area (100 million hectares)	Forest standing stock (100 million cubic meters)	Total standing stock (100 million cubic meters)	Cumulative total amount of carbon dioxide absorbed (100 million tons)
1948	8.60	0.828	90.28		165.21
1950–1962	11.81	1.13	110.24		201.74
1973–1976	12.70	1.22	86.6	95.32	158.48
1977–1981	12.00	1.15	90.3	102.61	165.25
1984–1988	12.98	1.25	91.41	105.72	167.28
1989–1993	13.92 (10.05)	1.33 (0.96)	106.7	119.50	195.26
1994–1999	16.55 (11.14)	1.59 (1.07)	112.7	124.90	206.24
1999–2003	18.21 (12.46)	1.75 (1.198)	124.56	136.18	227.94
2004–2009	20.36 (12.53)	1.95 (1.20)	137.21	149.13	251.09
2015	21.5	2.11	143	157.3	261.7
2020	23	2.21	150	163.9	272.7
2030	25	2.40	160	176	292.8

Note: Data in brackets are natural forests

Sources: Data for 1973–2009 were sourced from the 1st to the 7th forest inventories; nationwide forestry inventories were carried out between 1950 and 1962, but as the method of survey was diversified and requirements were not unified, the data could not reflect the real situation at the time. The data only serves as a reference. The 6th forest inventory included newly added forests during the inventory intervals. Data for 1948–2015 were sourced from the State Forestry Administration, "Study on Overview of China's Sustainable Forestry Strategy", p. 47, Beijing, China Forestry Publishing House; the planning and fund management department of the State Forestry Administration, and the economic development center of the State Forestry Administration, numerical interpretation of the forestry development during the 10th five-year plan period; the figures for the 7th National Forest Inventory and the 4th National Forest Inventory are the estimates of the author; the calculation method for total CO_2 sink is the years' forest stock × 1.83 tons/cubic meters (IPCC Special Report 2000: the growth of trees for each cubic meter can absorb 1.83 tons of carbon dioxide). Data for 2020 and 2030 are the estimates of the author, in reference to the national plan for major functional areas (December 2010)

The water crisis has become China's biggest crisis and the water issue is of greatest concern. Climate change has exacerbated China's water crisis, has led to an increase in extreme weather and has produced major changes in water sources and water hazards, which are increasing in frequency and intensity. The associated uncertainties and risks have also increased. The 2010 floods caused a direct economic loss of 350.5 billion yuan, the greatest so far this century.

The Central No.1 Document for 2011 focused on water conservancy, indicating that China's water issues have been placed high on the agenda. A meeting of the Central Water Conservancy Works proposed the implementation of a stringent water source management system, to speed up water source control, utilization and water utilization efficiency, and to establish three red lines (critical marks) for discharging pollution. The first is a red line to control the total amount of water used, limiting the use of water to 635 billion cubic meters by 2015, and 670 billion cubic meters by 2020. The second is a red line to ensure water use efficiency, with water consumption per 10,000 yuan added value in industry to reduce by more than 30% by 2015, with a further significant reduction by 2020. In addition, the effective utilization coefficient of irrigation water will increase by more than 0.55. The third red line is pollution control in functional areas, which strictly controls the total amount of pollutants discharged into rivers. By 2015, over 60 % of China's major rivers and lakes will meet the prescribed standards.[13]

The Central No. 1 Document and the convocation of the Central Water Conservancy Conference served as a harbinger of a golden age for water conservancy development from 2010 to 2015.[14] It is expected that water conservancy will enjoy a comprehensive and coordinated period of development between 2021 and 2030. China aims to realize its modernization of water conservancy by 2030, attaining a level compatible with China's high income, and realizing harmony between man and water. The development period is detailed below.

1. **Highly efficient and intensive utilization of water sources, delinking economic growth from water consumption.** Conservative estimates place China with "zero growth" in the sense of a balanced supply and demand by 2030. With the red line drawn, we hold that such a goal may be achieved ahead of time, probably between 2020 and 2025. The delinking of economic growth from water consumption is an important hallmark for realizing the green modernization of water conservancy. The effective utilization coefficient of irrigation water could increase to 0.55 by 2020 and to 0.6 by 2030, close to the level of 0.8 in developed countries. Water consumption per 10,000 yuan of industrial value added will drop by half, from 105 cubic meters in 2010 to 50 cubic meters by 2030, close to the level of developed countries.

---

[13] The national water consumption red line is locked at 670 billion cubic meters, Economic Reference News, July 22, 2011.

[14] The Central Water Conference identified the improvement of water conservancy construction within 5 to 10 years as a main objective for water conservancy work.

Table 8.2 Main indicators of China's water development (2000–2050)

Index	2000	2010	2015	2020	2030	2050	Developed countries reference values
Urban and rural domestic water supply coverage (%)	56	65	80	95	100	100	100
Effective utilization coefficient of irrigation water	0.43	0.5	0.53	0.55	0.6	0.8	0.8
Wan Yuan industrial value added water (cubic meters)	251	105	80	60	50	<50	<50
Share of water for ecological use in water total (%)	0	2	3	5	8	10	>10
Natural wetlands protection rate (%)	42	50	60	70	90	100	>95
Water quality of main rivers and lakes of water function areas of compliance (%)	40.8	47.4	60	80	95	100	>95
Soil and water loss area ratio (%)	38	37	34	31	25	15	<15

Sources: China Study Center of the Tsinghua University (project leader: Hu Angang and Wang Yahua; operators: Wang Yahua and Hu Angang): Study on the Water Conservancy Development Phase – Stage Classification, Evaluation And Development Of Water Resources Strategy Studies, March 2011

2. **The ecological environment of China's rivers and lakes will be significantly improved with the establishment of a protection system.** By 2020, the water quality of major rivers, lakes, and reservoirs will increase by approximately 80%.[15] Water use to improve the ecosystem will increase from its current rate of 2 to 5% by 2020, and to 8% by 2030. Protection of China's natural wetlands will rise from the current rate of 50 to 70% by 2020, and to 90% by 2030. Areas suffering from water loss and soil erosion will drop from 37 to 31% by 2020, and to 25% by 2030 (see Table 8.2)

By 2015, China will be able to ensure high-quality water for all. Issues surrounding rural drinking water will be essentially eliminated by 2015—China's 600 million rural residents will have safe drinking water. In 2010, urban and rural water supply coverage was 65%. This will increase to 95% by 2020 and to 100% by 2030, and a substantial proportion of the population will be able to directly access drinking water. This marks the modernization of drinking water for more than one billion people.

---

[15] "National Program of Main Function Zoning", December 2010.

3. **The impact of floods and drought on economic and social development will
   be reduced.** China's capacity for disaster prevention and mitigation will be
   further improved. The direct economic losses caused by floods and drought
   will drop from 1% of GDP to 0.5% of GDP to reach the level of developed
   countries.

However, as the modernization of water conservancy in China will still be in its
infancy, a conflict between China's vast population and limited water resources will
remain in 2030. China will not achieve full harmony between man and water until
2031–2050, with the modernization of China's water conservancy.

A Country with Clear Water and Blue Sky

Pollution has long undermined China's beautiful homeland, on which the Chinese
nation relies for survival. This is a long-term challenge and a factor that has
significantly constrained China's development. Since the 11th five-year plan period,
the environment has been improving with a noticeable reduction in the discharge
of pollutants. This made it possible, in 2005, to delink pollutants discharge from economic growth. The quality of China's air and water has been significantly improved.

As China is continuing to promote the construction of an environmentally
friendly society, environmental quality will steadily improve. The first step is to
reduce the discharge of pollutants to below the environment's capacity for self-
purification and the second step is to significantly improve the environment, ensuring
blue skies, clear water, and green mountains.

By 2030, there will be a significant reduction in the discharge of major pollutants, giving shape to a low-pollution and low-discharge production system, with
COD and SO_2 emissions to be reduced to less than 1,500 tons and 8.5 million tons,
respectively, and the discharge of ammonia-nitrogen and NO_2 emissions further
reduced. China's solid waste disposal rate will reach 90% and the sewage treatment
rate will reach 95%.

By 2030, the quality of China's ecological environment will have markedly
improved, with the establishment of an environmental protection system and an
environmentally friendly society. China's major environment quality indicators will
equal that of developed countries. Water within state controlled sections of China's
seven major waterways will be above Class III standards and their proportion will
reach 80%. The proportion of seawater of first and second class standards will
increase to 85%. The percentage of cities with Class II air quality will reach 97%.

By 2030, China will have established an eco-society, achieving the harmonious
co-existence of man and nature. Production and consumption will develop harmoni-
ously with China's natural ecosystems. A resource-efficient growth model and a
healthy and smart consumption model will prevail. The chosen industrial structure
and growth and consumption models will use less energy and resources, and favor
environmental protection. Having achieved harmony between environmental

Table 8.3 China's main resource consumption and pollution emissions and expected year of delinking (2000–2030)

Index	2000	2005	2010	2015	2020	2030	Delinking year
SO$_2$ emission (tons)	1,995.1	2,549.4	2,185.1	2,037.2	1,800	1,500	2005
COD (tons)	1,445	1,414	1,238.1	1,175.3	1,050	850	2005
Total amount of water used (100 million cubic meters)	5,530	5,633	5,998	6,350	6,700	6,500	2020
Coal consumption (100 million tons of standard coal)	10.07	16.71	23.04	24.92	27.88	25	2025

Note: Delinking year refers to the year when resource consumption and pollutant emissions begin to decline with economic growth
Sources: State Statistical Bureau (2003); State Statistical Bureau (2011b); data for 2020 and 2030 are the estimates of the author

protection and economic development, it will be possible for the delinking of economic growth from the consumption of major resources and the discharge of major pollutants (see Table 8.3). Thus, the environmental cost of economic and social development will be minimized, and optimal ecological and social benefits, and economic efficiency will be achieved by a unified arrangement of life, ecology, and production. Thus, long-lasting development and environmental protection will keep in step with economic and social development.

Concerted Efforts to Make China a Beautiful Homeland[16]

> This land so rich in beauty,
>   Has made countless heroes bow in homage. (Mao Zedong 2003)

In 1939, Mao Zedong sang the praises of the Chinese nation's fine homes in warm-hearted touches of the pen,

> China is one of the largest countries in the world, her territory being about the size of the whole of Europe. In this vast country of ours there are large areas of fertile land which provide us with food and clothing; mountain ranges across its length and breadth with extensive forests and rich mineral deposits; many rivers and lakes which provide us with water transport and irrigation; and a long coastline which facilitates communication with nations beyond the seas. From ancient times our forefathers have labored, lived and multiplied on this vast territory (Mao Zedong 1991).

The condition of China's land and its spatial ecological environment improved during the 11th five-year plan period, with forest cover increasing to 20.36%. In addition, China's natural ecological reserves have been offered protection and

---

[16] This section mainly refers to the areas under the main function zoning program (Dec. 2010); the author participated in the background study and it was used as a reference for related departments.

the natural wetland protection rate rose from 45% in 2005 to 49.6%. Ecological degradation has also gradually reduced, with reductions in water loss and soil erosion, grassland degradation, and desertification. The process of salinization in some areas has also been halted.

Over the next few decades, increases in total population, improvements in living standards, progress in urbanization and industrialization, and the construction of China's modern infrastructure, will bring a great demand for land and space accompanied by significant ecological pressure. We must designate key functional zones and develop our homes using scientific methods to ensure beautiful but economical houses, greater coordinated regional development, greater prosperity and harmony for China's people; thus, we can leave our children and grandchildren bluer skies, greener homes, and clearer water.[17]

Scientific development represents the comprehensive scientific evaluation of land and space based on our basic natural geographical conditions, which include national land resources, water resources, environmental capacity, and the vulnerability and importance of ecosystems. Such evaluations also include the aftermath of natural disasters, population concentration, economic development levels, communications, and transport benefits. As a result, scientific development is characterized by top-level design. The National Plan on Main Functional Zones (Dec. 2010) is a program of action and offers a long-range blueprint for the scientific development of China's land and space. It is a binding elementary strategic plan, aimed at constructing an efficient, coordinated, and sustainable land and spatial development pattern.

Within the next 20 years, China will establish an extensive "two screens and three belts" strategic ecological security pattern. The two screens are the Qinghai-Tibet Plateau ecological screen and the Loess Plateau-Sichuan-Yunnan ecological screen; the three belts are the northeast-north-northwest shelter belt, the northeast China forest belt, and the south China hill and mountain belt. These screens and belts will divide stock and crop farming areas and the transitional areas of the three gradients, using large rivers and waterways as a framework. Restrictions or bans will be imposed in terms of development, water sources, sandstorm prevention, sand fixation, soil and water conservation, biological diversity, and the protection of natural resources. The ecological roles of the national key ecological function areas[18] will increase significantly. The zones where development is banned will become important areas to protect natural and cultural resources, endangered animals, and plant genetic resources.[19]

---

[17] "National main functional zone planning", December 21, 2010.

[18] Key national ecological function areas include 25 areas, such as the Lesser Xing'an and the mountain forest ecological function zone, covering approximately 3.86 million square kilometers, which is 40.2% of the country's land area, with a population accounting for 8.5% of China's then 1.1 billion people.

[19] The zones where development is banned refer to representative natural ecosystems, natural concentrations of rare and endangered species of wild flora and fauna, locations that have natural and cultural sites of significance, and key ecological functional zones where industrialization and urbanization are banned. According to the laws, regulations and relevant provisions, there are 1,443 zones where development is banned, covering a total area of approximately 1.20 million

This is an ambitious and bold plan to restructure China's mountains and rivers to establish a healthy ecosystem. It represents the most up-to-date and beautiful vision for 9.60 million square kilometers of land. Once contemporary China completes its great process of industrialization and modernization, this plan will offer a precious and green legacy for future generations.

In the next 20 years, China will have a clearer pattern regarding its land and space and its ecosystems will be more stable. It will maintain and expand its green space to provide ecological assets, ecological services, and ecological security. Forest stock will increase to 3.12 million square kilometers and the proportion of grassland in the total land area will be maintained at over 40%. In addition, rivers, lakes, and wetland areas will increase.[20] The proportion of areas experiencing ecological degradation will reduce and cultivated land will not exceed 120 million hectares. This represents the red line safeguard for the supply of agricultural products, which includes 104 million hectares of basic farmland. Areas left for future industrialization and urbanization development and other construction purposes will equal just 280,000 km^2, approximately 3% of the total land area. This is a space-efficient and intensive development path, with the unit areas designed to achieve maximum production values and the population density of cities to significantly increase.[21]

By 2020, the national main functional zone distribution will have taken shape;[22] by 2030, the national ecological security screen system will be established. The Chinese nation will live in a homeland characterized by highly intensive and efficient production spaces, comfortable living spaces, eco-spaces with green mountains and clear water, and a coordinated development system of population, economy, resources, and environment (Fig. 8.1).

World's Largest Green Energy Nation

Energy problems have caused the greatest bottleneck in China's long-term development. China is already the biggest energy producer and consumer in the world. In 2010, China ranked first in the world with its primary energy production reaching 2.99 billion tons and a primary energy consumption of 3.25 billion tons (State Statistical Bureau 2011a).

Over the next 20 years, China will still be in a stage of rapid development in terms of industrialization and urbanization, and as a result, China will continue to be the world's greatest "superpower" in energy production and consumption, and in

---

square kilometers or 12.5% of the country's land area. China's national nature reserve, cultural and natural heritage, state-level scenic areas, national parks, and future national geological parks will automatically enter the directory of the development-ban areas. The National Plan on Main Functional Zones (December 2010).

[20] Green spaces includes forests, grassland, wetland, and water surface.

[21] National Plan on Main Functional Zones, December 21, 2010.

[22] National Plan on Main Functional Zones, December 21, 2010.

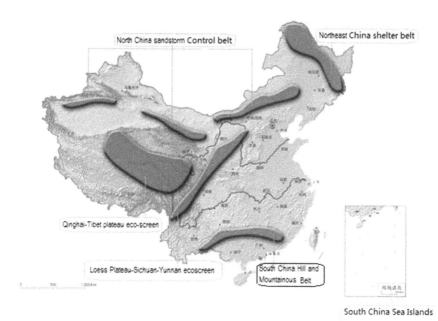

Fig. 8.1 "Two screens and three belts" ecological security strategic pattern (Source: 12th Five-Year National Economic and Social Development Program of the People's Republic of China, March 2011)

Table 8.4 World's total energy demand for five major world economies (1980–2030)

Unit: %

	1980	2000	2008	2015	2020	2030
United States	24.93	22.63	18.59	16.55	15.73	14.29
EU	n.a	16.77	14.25	12.50	11.84	10.73
Japan	4.77	5.17	4.04	3.59	3.37	3.01
Russia	n.a	6.18	5.61	5.15	5.05	4.88
China	8.34	11.04	17.37	16.60	21.70	22.28
India	2.88	4.58	5.05	5.65	6.21	7.52
World	100.00	100.00	100.00	100.00	100.00	100.00

Sources: International Energy Agency (2010)

coal production and consumption. China's significant population size effect and economic scale effect (because of its rapid growth) are sure to give rise to large-scale energy consumption. According to IEA forecasts, China's energy consumption will represent 22.3% of the world's total by 2030, close to that of the United States (14.3%) and the Eu (10.7%) combined (see Table 8.4).

However, we must not lose sight of the fact that even though China's energy consumption will be 1.6 times that of the United States by 2030, it will still be lower

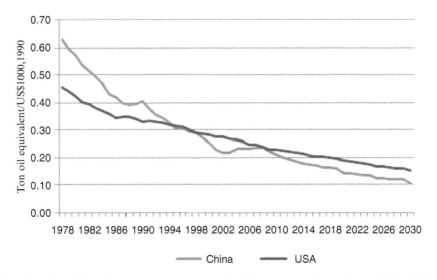

Fig. 8.2 Unit GDP (PPP) energy consumption for China and the United States (1978–2030) (Sources: Data for 1978–2010 were sourced from Angus Maddison, *Historical Statistics for the World Economy: 1–2008 AD*; World Bank, World Development Indicator 2010; data for 2010–2030 are the author's calculations)

than the economic aggregate ratio of the two countries (2.2–2.5 times lower) and lower than their total population ratio (4 times lower).

The path of China's energy consumption is one that will change from excessive consumption to moderate consumption, from extensive to intensive use, and from black energy to green energy.

In the next 20 years, China's energy utilization efficiency will improve, becoming more efficient and intensive than the United States. In fact, since the reform and opening up, China's energy utilization efficiency has continued to improve, with unit GDP energy consumption dropping steadily. Compared with 1978, unit GDP energy consumption has declined by 73%. We estimate that by 2020, it will reduce further by 35% and 55.4% by 2030. From a perspective of international comparison and calculated using PPP, China's energy utilization efficiency will continue to rise, far faster than the worldwide rate for the same period. China's 1978 unit GDP energy consumption was 1.4 times that of the United States. However, by 2000, it was already at levels similar to the United States. It took China only 50 years to complete the transition from extensive to intensive energy use, whereas it took the United States 100 years. In the next 20 years, China's economy will maintain a high growth rate while under the constraint of energy consumption, and under China's development plan, energy consumption growth will remain low. China's unit GDP energy consumption will be lower than that of the United States for a long time to come and China will lead the United States in its energy utilization rate. By 2030, China's unit GDP energy consumption will be just 70 % of the United States' (see Fig. 8.2).

Table 8.5 World total percentages of non-fossil energy consumption for four major world economies (1980–2030)

Unit: %

	1980	1990	2000	2006	2015	2020	2030
China	4.0	5.1	6.4	6.8	12	18	26
United States	8.5	13.5	13.9	14.3	16	17	20
Japan	8.6	15.3	19.2	18.4	19	20	22
Europe	8.7	20	22.6	23.6	20	20	23

Sources: World Bank, World Development Indicator 2011; data for 2015–2030 are the calculations of the author in reference to the target values of various economies

By 2030, China will become the world's largest green energy investor, producer, consumer, exporter, the largest producer of new energy technologies and equipment, and the largest exporter.

China is fully capable of becoming a leader in the following round of the green industrial revolution because of its huge domestic market. China's resolute political decision-making, highly efficient investments, and effective application of political power will enable it to become dominant in the green revolution. In addition, China will lead the way by developing low-carbon technologies, green innovations, and its application of emission-reducing technology.

China will become the world's leader in green energy, and will optimize its energy structure: (1) to improve its proportion of non-fossil energy sources in total energy consumption, especially the proportion of solar energy, wind, and other renewable energy forms; (2) to reduce its share of coal in fossil energy consumption; (3) to use clean coal throughout its technological transformation. China's national 12th five-year plan established the goal of increasing the proportion of non-fossil energy consumption in total energy consumption to 11.2%. According to the 2009 goal of the State Council, the proportion of renewable energy in total energy consumption will reach 15% by 2020. We estimate that this goal will be attained ahead of time. By 2015, China's share of non-fossil energy will reach 12% and 19% by 2020, and increase again to 26%,[23] outstripping the United States and the EU. China will become one of the world's highest users of green energy[24] (see Table 8.5).

China will become the world leader in the development of new energy sources, clean energy, and low-carbon industries. The International Energy Agency (IEA) published the World Energy Outlook 2010, and predicted under its "new policy" scenario that the global demand for natural gas will grow 1.4% annually between

---

[23] This a relatively conservative estimate. The CAS forecast 20% by 2020 and up to 34% by 2030 (see Chinese Academy of Sciences 2009).

[24] Countries around the world have enacted 2020 clean energy (non-fossil energy) development plans and objectives. Germany's goal is the most ambitious, planning to bring its clean energy share in total energy consumption to 30%, followed by the European Union and the United States, both setting a goal of 20%. However, it will be very difficult to achieve such objectives.

2008 and 2035. It stated that China's demand will grow the fastest, reaching 6%, and its share in the global growth of total demand will reach 23%. Further, it states that "China is likely to lead the world into a golden age of natural gas."

China will also obtain substantial achievements in renewable energy development. Between 2008 and 2035, China's demand for renewable energy will account for 20 % of the global growth and it will become one of the three major economies with the greatest demands for renewable energy. We have reason to believe that, thanks to the size of its population and economic growth potential, China will, in the not too distant future, overtake the United States and the EU to become the world's largest renewable energy consumer.

China's huge domestic market and investment demand will spur the rapid development of low-carbon technologies. China has become the leader in wind power and photovoltaic power production and the world's leading supplier of related equipment. Compared with other areas that also have significant potential in solar energy development (for example the Middle East and North Africa), China enjoys the advantage of the size of its market, technical levels, and political stability. According to the IEA's "Outlook," by 2035 China will represent 19%, 26%, 29%, and 21% of the world's growth in solar power, wind power, nuclear power, and electric and hybrid vehicles, respectively.

A Country of Low-Carbon Green Development

In the twenty-first century, the world will launch an unprecedented energy and environmental revolution, aimed at encouraging economic growth and delinking carbon emissions from economic growth (which will peak by 2020 before a rapid and large-scale decline). International organizations have a global goal of emission reduction and a roadmap to limit the concentration of atmospheric greenhouse gases to 450 ppm and the global temperature to 2 °C. Thus, they hope to achieve the long-term stabilization of the global climate and avoid a widespread ecological disaster.[25]

Despite the concerted efforts of more than 200 countries to realize the roadmap for the reduction of global emissions, the relationship between China and the rest of the world in terms of emissions reduction shows that the success of the reduction is largely up to China. This is because China has the biggest influence on global emissions, at a level greater than the United States, the EU, India, and any other populous

---

[25] According to Oxfam's latest research, between 1997 and 2008 global climate change affected on average 278 million people annually and this number will increase by 45% to reach 375 million by 2015. This will pose serious challenges to the global humanitarian disaster relief system. An IPCC report also said that in the next 10 years, at least 200 million people in Latin America, Asia, and Africa will experience a shortage of safe drinking water. By the middle of the century, an additional 130 million people in Asia will be threatened by hunger. By 2100, Africa's crop revenue will be reduced by 90%.

developing countries. Therefore, China's success in emissions reduction represents a success for the world and China's failure represents a worldwide failure.[26] Thus, China must succeed, and the earlier the emissions peak, the better and the lower the emission peaks, the better. Furthermore, the sooner that economic growth is delinked from carbon emissions, and the lower the delinking point, the better.

The general concept for a green China is "one world, one dream, one (emissions) action, and keeping pace with the rest of the world regarding emissions". We also need to include the management of climate change in China's modernization process. Green modernization is an inevitable road for China and its long-term economic growth will not be affected by the management of climate change via a green economy, the adjustment of the industrial structure, the development of green industries, investment in green energy, and the promotion of green consumption. On the contrary, it will greatly improve the quality of China's economic growth and social welfare, thus achieving multiple progress in economic development, environmental protection, ecological safety, and adaptation to climate change. At the same time, as the country with the largest population, economic aggregate, and the greatest number of innovation patents, China will make major contributions toward achieving the "stable 450 ppm" scenario and reduce greenhouse gases by half through the peaceful development of green technology and international cooperation.[27]

Thus, we have described China's "green cat" roadmap, which mirrors that of the world. By 2020, carbon emissions will reach its peak at approximately 8.0 billion tons (carbon equivalent). Compared with the "black cat" model, it will reduce emissions by 1.5 billion tons (carbon equivalent). By 2030, it will drop to 6–7 billion tons (carbon equivalent). Compared with the "black cat" model, the "green cat" model represents a reduction of approximately five billion tons (carbon equivalent). In addition, the Energy Institute of the State Development and Reform Commission holds that with China's increasing dependency on clean energy, CO_2 emissions are likely to peak around 2030.

If we follow the existing emissions reduction roadmap and trends, there will be no way of ensuring that China's emissions reach their peak value in 10–15 years. However, if we regard the Chinese government's emissions reduction plan as a trend variable and add a series of "acceleration variables," such as policy incentives, technological innovation, and opening up, it may be possible for China to realize its peak value of emissions between 2020 and 2030.

We consider that China's CO_2 emissions in the next 20 years will lie somewhere between the 2020 peak value scheme and the 2030 peak value scheme. We have estimated (according to the worst case scenario situation using the 2030 peak value)

---

[26] Emission reduction means intervention activities to reduce greenhouse gas emissions or to enhance carbon sink. This is achieved via a green economy, green energy, and forestry developments, the rational use of land and an increase in carbon sink capacity.

[27] In order to ensure that the global temperature increase would not exceed 2 °C, it is necessary to reduce greenhouse gas emissions by 25–40% as compared with 1990 levels, and realize the goal of cutting total emissions by 50% by 2050 (Yang Jiemian 2009).

Table 8.6 World total percentages for carbon dioxide emissions by China, the United States and EU (1990–2030)

Unit: %				
Nation	1990	2007	2020	2030
China	10.7	21.1	26.1	24.9
United States	23.1	19.9	15.8	13.8
EU	19.3	13.5	10.2	8.7

Source: Data for the United States and EU were sourced from the IEA, World Energy Outlook 2010; data for China are the author's estimates

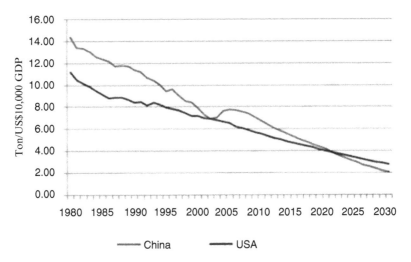

Fig. 8.3 China and the United States GDP (PPP) of carbon dioxide emissions (1980–2030) (Note: GDP data for the PPP constant prices (1990 International Geary-Khamis dollars). Calculating data sources: Angus Maddison. *Historical Statistics of the World Economy: 1-2008 AD;* carbon dioxide emissions data from CDIAC (Carbon Dioxide Information Analysis Center), 18-Jan-2011;2010-2030 Annual author's estimates)

that by 2030, China will be the No. 1 CO_2 emitter in the world. However, when China's economic aggregate is at least two times that of the United States, China's CO_2 emissions will be only 1.8 times that of the United States (see Table 8.6)

At the same time, China's carbon emission intensity will be significantly lower than that of the United States. China's unit GDP CO_2 emissions peaked in 1977 and has been in decline ever since. By 2009, it was 7.01 tons per US$10,000 of GDP. By 2030, it will be 2.06 tons per US$10,000, significantly lower than the United States (see Fig. 8.3)

China, like the United States, is in the process of becoming the world's largest economy. Inevitably, it will also become the world's largest energy consumer and CO_2

emitter. However, China's unit GDP energy consumption, unit GDP CO_2 emissions, per capita energy consumption and CO_2 emissions, and cumulative energy consumption and CO_2 emissions, will always be lower than the United States. China, as a new type of "superpower" (as compared with a traditional "superpower" like the United States), will be much greener in terms of its development model, with a lower level of negative externalities and a higher level of green positive externalities.

At the same time, China will complete the building of its new low disaster risk society,[28] and reduce the economic vulnerability of society in its management of natural disasters. The number of deaths caused by natural disasters will drop significantly and the direct economic losses in GDP will markedly decrease (to less than 0.5%).[29] The number of deaths caused by natural disasters will be close to the level of developed countries and the average annual death toll from natural disasters will drop to 0.3 persons/million people.

Summary: Toward Green Modernization

China's road toward modernization is one of innovation. Its development model is different from traditional development models that feature the shared growth of both the economy and greenhouse gases since the British industrial revolution in 1750.[30] Instead, in the first half of the twenty-first century, China created a new green development model featuring the simultaneous decline of economic growth and greenhouse gas emissions, and even the delinking of economic growth from greenhouse gas emissions.

The themes of China's modernization are green development and scientific development; that is, from black industrialization, urbanization, and modernization to green industrialization, urbanization, and modernization; a shift from black to green in terms of manufacturing, energy, trade, cities, consumption.

---

[28] This includes the "four abilities:" a disaster monitoring and early warning capacity; a comprehensive disaster prevention ability; comprehensive disaster emergency response and management abilities; and disaster relief and restoration capabilities.

[29] Between 2007 and 2008, China's natural disasters caused 91,253 deaths. The number of people evacuated from their homes and resettled was 4,181.3, 3.15% of the total population. Crop disasters affected 8,898.3 million hectares, of which, 9.779 million hectares produced a zero yield, accounting for 55.9% and 6.3% of the total sowing areas, respectively. In addition, 12.444 million houses collapsed. The direct economic loss came to 1,411.54 billion yuan, equivalent to 2.53% of two years' GDP, substantially higher than the national integrated disaster mitigation target set in the 11th five-year plan, which was to limit direct economic losses within 1.5% of GDP.

[30] IEA report points out that between 1750 and 2007, the global GDP dollar value and carbon emissions assumed an upward trend. IEA, 2009, "The Impact of the Financial and Economic Crisis on Global Energy Investment", May 2009.

Thus, the green modernization of China can be implemented in three steps.[31]

The first step (2006–2020) is to reduce CO_2 emissions and to adapt to climate change. By about 2020, CO_2 emissions will reach their peak.[32] According to IEA data, China's energy related CO_2 emissions measured 2.244 billion tons in 1990 and 5.684 billion tons in 2006. China will strive to control CO_2 emissions to eight billion tons by 2020 (even so, China's CO_2 emissions will account for approximately 20 % of the world's total). This requires that China significantly reduce the rate of emissions within the 12th five-year plan period (2011–2015). Then, by the 13th five-year plan period (2016–2020), emissions should stabilize and peak. At that time, the percentage of agriculture in GDP will be approximately 8%. The percentage of industries will drop to 38% and the service industry will increase to 47%. The urban population will represent 57% of the population. The percentage of renewable energy shares will be close to or reach 20% and coal consumption will drop to less than 60%. The level of clean coal use and technology will be high and forest cover will be at 23%. China's patent applications will rank third in the world, GDP will rank second, and GDP (PPP) will rank first.[33]

The second step (2020–2030) is to enter a CO_2 reduction stage. By 2030, China's CO_2 emissions will significantly reduce, striving to reach the levels of 2005.[34] By that time, the percentage of China's agriculture in GDP will be just 5%, 30% for industry, and 60% for the service industry. The urban population will be 65% of China's total population. Renewable energy will be greater than 25% and coal consumption between 45% and 50%. Levels of clean coal utilization will be high and forest cover will reach 24%. China's applications for patents will rank second in the world and China's GDP and GDP (PPP) will be the highest worldwide.

---

[31] Here we have followed Deng Xiaoping's three-step strategy for China's modernization, when he said, "By the end of this century China's per capita GNP will reach between US $800 and $1,000 - we have hopes that it will be $1,000. I am afraid that China will still rank below 50th place among the more than 100 countries in the world, but there will be a difference in its strength. Our population will have reached 1.2 to 1.25 billion, and total GNP will be between $1 trillion and $1.2 trillion. Since our socialist system is based on public ownership, and since our goal is to achieve common prosperity, we shall then have a society in which the people lead a fairly comfortable life -- that is, everyone's standard of living will have been raised. More important, if with this as a foundation we can continue to develop, in another 50 years we shall again quadruple our per capita GNP to $4,000. This will put China among the moderately developed countries, though its place will still be lower than that of dozens of others. At that time, with a population of 1.5 billion producing a GNP of $6 trillion (calculated in accordance with the 1980 exchange rate of the renminbi yuan against the U.S. dollar), China will surely be in the front ranks of the countries of the world. And thanks to our socialist system of distribution, not only will there be a change in China's national strength, but the people's standard of living will be higher."

[32] According to IEA estimates, the greenhouse gas emissions of OECD countries will reach its peak in 2015 before beginning to decline (IEA 2007).

[33] It also shows that, the implementation of emission reduction targets will not affect China's goal of realizing a prosperous society by 2020. China will not only rank first in terms of economic aggregate but also among the high-level group regarding HDI.

[34] According to IEA data, China's CO_2 emissions equaled 2.2 billion tons in 1990 and increased to 5.2 billion tons. (IEA 2007).

The third step (2030–2050) represents a significant reduction in CO_2 emissions by 2050, keeping in step with the rest of the world to meet half of the 1990 levels.[35] By that time, China's agriculture will contribute to 2%–3% of GDP and industry will account for less than 20% of GDP. The percentage of the service industry will be close to 80% and the urban population rate will be at 78%. The percentage of renewable energy will be greater than 55% and coal consumption will drop to 25%–30%. Clean energy will be used throughout China. Forest cover will reach 26% and China will submit the largest number of patent applications worldwide. Essentially, China's green modernization will be achieved, reaching the level of developed countries. China will truly contribute to the green development of humanity worldwide.[36]

By 2030, China will enter a period of comprehensive ecological surplus. First, economic growth will be delinked from energy consumption, fossil fuel consumption, CO_2 emissions, water consumption, and pollutants discharge. Second, humanity will nurture nature, with an improvement in China's environmental quality, and there will be a substantial increase in the area of forests, grasslands, wetlands, and other ecological assets. Thus, China's age-old ideal of unity between heaven and man will be fully realized. Human development will no longer be at the cost of nature and man and nature will co-exist. This will be of great significance to China's future development and the greatest contribution to human civilization; that is, China's green contribution and the "unity of man and nature" (see Box 8.1)

Box 8.1 Unity of Man and Nature—Green Development'

Western cultures believe that humanity is the master of all things. Humanity can control and tame nature, and make it serve humanity.[37] With the development of science, such ideas have been greatly been advanced. However, the relationship between man and nature has come to represent a paradox. On the one hand, man has possessed an unprecedented capability to transform nature; on the other hand, humanity has experienced the unprecedented destructive revenge of nature.

continued

---

[35] An IPCC (2007) report stated that by 2050 greenhouse gas density will be maintained at 445–490 ppm for a long period and global greenhouse gas emissions will be reduced by half as compared with 1990.

[36] On the morning of April 26, 1987, Deng Xiaoping said during his meeting with Premier Lubomir Strougal of the Czechoslovak Socialist Republic that by the middle of the next century we hope to reach the level of the moderately developed countries. If we can achieve this goal, first, we shall have accomplished a tremendous task; second, we shall have made a real contribution to mankind; and third, we shall have demonstrated more convincingly the superiority of the socialist system (Central Documentation Research 2004).

[37] The Bible says: "And God said, Let us make man in our image, after our likeness: and let them have dominion over the fish of the sea, and over the fowl of the air, and over the cattle, and over all the earth, and over every creeping thing that creepeth upon the earth." The Bible, "Genesis".

Box 8.1 (contiuned)

China's traditional wisdom believes that man is an integral part of nature. Since ancient times, the Chinese have endeavored not to betray nature and have instead tried to live in harmony with the environment (Qian Mu 1990). Chinese culture has a natural respect for nature and is very close to it. In recent years, a noted scholar of the Chinese culture, Mr. Rao Zongyi, has developed the idea of "man being an integral part of nature." Based on Yi Jing, he put forward the idea of learning wisdom from the cultures of the ancients, not to harm nature (and vice versa) but to create an environment of mutual benefit between man and nature. Thus, achieving the realm of "man and nature vying with each other to stay on" as described by the poet Su Shi.[38]

Drawing on such traditional wisdom, we have put forward the idea of green development, that is, an economic and social development model of low consumption and low emissions, and an increase in ecological capital (Hu Angang and Wu Yilong 2010). This model counters the limitations of human-centered "sustainable development,"[39] showing the way for humanity in the twenty-first century, which is to seek a green development path toward fusion and co-existence, and common prosperity between man and nature.

Green development is divided into three stages. The first stage is to narrow the gap between man and nature, reducing the ecological deficit, breaking the cycle of mutual harm between man and nature. The second stage is to close the gap between man and nature and to bring the ecological account into balance, realizing man and nature living in harmony. The third stage is to back feed nature, creating a surplus in the ecological account to achieve the goal of mutual benefit between man and nature and to create a realm where man and nature co-exist for common prosperity.

Green development has five pillars to support: a resource-efficient society, an environmentally friendly society, an ecological surplus society, a society that has achieved climate adaptation, and a low disaster risk society. These five pillars lead to a harmonious relationship with nature and ultimately common prosperity.

Modern Western civilizations strive to control nature to meet their desires, and therefore create unprecedented challenges trying to achieve their development miracles. The oriental wisdom of the "unity of man and nature" and green development will no doubt dilute such Western notions.

continued

---

[38]. "Not only must man and nature live in harmony, but they must mutually benefit each other", Nanfang Daily, Nov. 18, 2009.

[39] The UN World Environment and Development Commission, in its "Our Common Future" April 1987, put forward the classical definition that sustainable development refers to satisfying the demand of the contemporary people without threatening the development abilities of the future generations to satisfy their demand, including resources and environment sustainability, social sustainability and economic sustainability.

Box 8.1 (contiuned)

Western philosopher Bertrand Russell stated, "The significant advantage of our civilization (western) lies in scientific method while the advantage of the Chinese civilization lies in the rational interpretation of the ultimate aim of people. People certainly hope to see their integration" (Russell 1996). Oriental philosopher Qian Mu commented that the "Harmony of man and nature is in fact the end of the traditional Chinese culture. I deeply believe that it is here that lies the contribution of Chinese culture to the future survival of humanity" (Qian Mu 1990).

References

Central Documentation Research Center (2004) Deng Xiaoping Chronicle (1975–1997), Part II. Central Documentation Press, Beijing, p 1182

Chinese Academy of Sciences (2009) The science and technology revolution and the modernization of China, Science Press, p 46

Hu Jintao (2011) Speech at the central work conference on water. Xinhua News Agency, Beijing, 9 July

Hu Angang, Wu Yilong (2010) China: toward 2015. Tsinghua University China Study Center/ Zhejiang People's Publishing House, p 131

Hu Angang, Wang Yi, Niu Wenyuan (1990) The ecological deficit: the biggest crisis in the survival of the Chinese nation in the 21st century, August 1989. Sci Technol Her (2 and 3)

International Energy Agency (2010) The World Energy Outlook 2010. IEA, Paris

Mao Zedong (1991) The Chinese revolution and the Chinese communist party, December 1939. In: Selected works of Mao Zedong, vol II. People's Publishing House, Beijing, pp 584–585

Mao Zedong's Poem (2003) "Snow", Feb. 1936. In Collection of Mao Zedong's Poems. CPC Central Documentation Office, Central Documentation Press, Beijing, p 56

Qian Mu (1990) The possible contributions of Chinese culture to the future of mankind. Xinye Monthly, Dec

Russell B (1996) The problem of China (trans: Qin Yue). Xuelin Publishing House, London, p 153

State Statistical Bureau (2003) China statistical yearbook. China Statistical Press, Beijing, p 852

State Statistical Bureau (2011a) China statistical abstract 2011. China Statistical Press, Beijing, p 141

State Statistical Bureau (2011b) China statistical digest. China Statistical Press, Beijing, p 141, and p 183

The Ecology and Environment Strategy Study Group of the Chinese Academy of Sciences (2009) Roadmap for ecological and environmental technology development up to 2050. Science Press, Beijing, pp 67–69

World Bank (2008) World development indicators 2008. China Financial and Economic Publishing House, Beijing, p 165

Yang Jiemian (ed) (2009) World climate diplomacy and China's countermeasures. Shishi Publishing House, Beijing, p 263

Chapter 9
Concerted Efforts Toward Great Harmony

I am deeply convinced that the future of China belongs to the Chinese people and the future of the world belongs to the people of the world.

Deng Xiaoping (1981)[1]

"The people, and the people alone, are the motive force in the making of world history" (Mao Zedong 1991). 'The people' refers to both Chinese people and the people of the world. These people are the real heroes; they have created both Chinese and world history. These are our elementary views and perspectives concerning China and the rest of the world, encompassing our dialectical and historical materialism.

In reviewing the past and looking to the future we can map China's path. In 1949, 540 million Chinese people rose up and sought change. In 1978, one billion Chinese people initiated China's reform and opening up. By 2000, 1.2 billion Chinese people created a prosperous society. By 2030, 1.4 billion Chinese people will achieve universal wealth. By 2050, 1.4 billion Chinese people will realize a high degree of modernization.

In June 1964, Mao Zedong said, "We must serve the interests of the overwhelming majority of the people, serve the interests of the overwhelming majority of the Chinese people and the overwhelming majority of the world people but not the minority" (Mao Zedong 1996).

This is the starting point and the ending point for us to both understand and transform China and to understand and transform the world.

---

[1] This is the foreword written by Deng Xiaoping on February 14, 1981 for the book *Speeches and writings: Deng Xiaoping* published by Pergamon Press Ltd (Central Documentation Office 2004).

A. Hu et al., *China 2030*, DOI 10.1007/978-3-642-31328-8_9,
© Springer-Verlag Berlin Heidelberg 2014

This chapter discusses the core theme of "great harmony." It is the central viewpoint of this book. It has two interrelated connotations. The first is a great harmonious China, referring to the more than one billion people making concerted efforts to build a wealthy society; the second is a great harmonious world, referring to the more than 200 countries and regions, and billions of people making concerted efforts to build a world of common prosperity. "Great harmony" is achieved by the elements of interest and destiny. China's population of more than one billion people and 56 nationalities is an interested community and a community of destiny. Their fundamental interests lie in the relentless pursuit of common prosperity and great harmony for China. Similarly, the billions of people worldwide, albeit with different motives, have long-term interests in a world of common prosperity and a world of great harmony.

China's great harmony requires worldwide great harmony and vice versa. Without great harmony in China, there would be no great harmony in the world; without great harmony in the world, there would be no true great harmony in China. This, we hold, is the key theme, dream and objective of both China and the world, for 2030 and beyond.

To follow is a summary of the book, highlighting the main research results and the perspectives of each chapter.

Common Wealth Society

1. **A large strong power with a population of more than one billion people**

   By 2030, China will become a strong economic power of more than one billion people. China will become a world economic power in its real sense. Before 2020, China will overtake the United States in terms of GDP aggregate, to be 1.0–1.7 times that of the United States, breaking its hold as the world's No. 1 for more than 100 years. By 2030, China's GDP aggregate will be 2.0–2.2 times that of the United States.[2]

   China will become the biggest consumer and import market, with its domestic market ranking first in the world, and by 2030 it will be 1.7–1.9 times that of the United States.

   China will boast the largest modern industrial system to become the world's leading power with modernized services. It will be an economy that will transition from an economy driven mainly by material factor (resources, labor and capital) inputs to an economy driven mainly by information, knowledge, and innovation. By 2030, China will outnumber the United States in terms of representation in the world's top 500 companies.

---

[2] What concerns us most is that the United States does not draw on the painful lessons of this financial crisis; it does not take the initiative to reform and reduce its growth. The GDP gap between China and the United State will continue to grow.

China will become the largest urbanized area in the world. By 2030, China's urbanization rate will reach 70%, presenting a unique pattern with two horizontal and three vertical city clusters that will cover the core areas of the country.

China will have the most modern infrastructure system in the world. Apart from its traditional rail system, China's main communications, energy and power, telecommunications and information, and other infrastructure networks will rank first in the world to form the largest, operational communication, transport, information, and telecommunications systems. These systems will be fully functioning, well managed, and interconnected.

2. **A country of innovation created by the concerted efforts by the more than one billion people**

China will become the most powerful country in terms of science, technology, and innovation, with its S&T power accounting for 20% of the world's total. In addition, China will account for 25% of published science papers worldwide, 35% of all patent applications, 25% of R&D inputs, and 30% of high-tech products exports.

China will become the largest power in terms of human resources, with its total human resources to exceed 25% of the world's total,[3] 3.9 times that of the United States, thus achieving huge education dividends.

China will become the biggest and strongest power in terms of competent personnel, with the total number of people of ability to reach 270 million,[4] accounting for approximately 33% of total employment, and R&D personnel will represent 33% of the world's total.

China will become the biggest ICT nation, with its Internet users to account for 33% of the world's total and the total number of mobile phone users to account for 25% of the world's total. China will become the biggest ICT producer and exporter.

3. **A country of common prosperity created cooperatively by China's population of more than one million people**

China will become a high-income country. According to calculations using three major methods (annual exchange dollar price, annual PPP dollar price, and PPP 1990 dollar price), China's per capita GDP will be 52–56% that of the United States.

China will become a country with a high level of education. By 2030, the expected years of education will be close to 18 years, exceeding the United States and realizing the modernization of the socialist education system with distinct Chinese characteristics. China will become a learning society in which all people engage in life-long and flexible learning.

China will become one of the healthiest countries in the world, with a mean life expectancy of 80 years, 1.4 years less than the United States. Some provinces, cities,

---

[3] Total human resources refers to the average years of education received by people aged 15 years and above plus the working age population (15–64 years of age).

[4] The total number of competent personnel refers to personnel working in the Party and government, specialized technical personnel, business managers, highly skilled people, practical rural personnel, and social workers combined. "Outlined Program for the Medium- and Long-term Development of Competent Personnel (2010–2020), Beijing, Xinhua (June 6, 2010) reports."

and regions will even catch up to and overtake the United States (81.3 years).[5] The healthy life expectancy will reach 75 years, 0.3 years less than the United States. All the other health indicators will reach the level of high-income countries.

China will become a country with a high level of human development, with its HDI to reach 0.776 to enter the top of the world rankings. China's HDI is likely to exceed 0.800 in the years 2040–2050, attaining an extremely high level of human development.

China will become the largest country in terms of GHDI. From 2010 to 2030, the GHDI ratio between China and the United States will be maintained at over three times higher than the ratio of economic aggregate.

All regional development disparities will be narrowed, with the coefficient of variation in the per capita development index to significantly reduce. The rural/urban development gap will be narrowed in all areas, with the convergence of the main per capita development index.

Various levels of regional and rural/urban public services will further converge. All of China's people will enjoy social security, with the world's largest and most advanced social security system to cover all rural and urban areas, all regions, and China's population groups.

4. **A beautiful homeland created by the concerted efforts of the more than one billion people**

China will become a country with the largest forested areas in the world. China's forest cover will reach 25% and its forest standing stock will reach 16 billion cubic meters. China will become the world's largest artificial forest carbon sink.

China will become a country characterized by its harmonious relationship between man and water. By approximately 2020, China will delink economic growth from water resources consumption, improve its hydro-ecology, and raise its main water resources indices close to those of developed countries.

China will become a country with clear waters and blue skies. By 2030, the total discharge of principal pollutants will be markedly reduced. The air quality will reach second-class standards in 97% of Chinese cities. Production systems will have low-level pollutant discharge. China's eco-environment will feature green hills, clear waters, and blue skies.

An impressive strategic pattern of eco-security will take shape with the implementation of the "two screens and three belts" system. China's land and space patterns will become clearer and its eco-system will become more stable. A nationwide eco-security screen system will be created. China will create numerous intensive and highly efficient production spaces, comfortable and appropriate living spaces, all under the harmonious development of population, economy, resources, and environment.

China will become the biggest country in terms of green energy, including the biggest green energy investor, producer, consumer, and exporter. Its non-fossil

---

[5] The mean life expectancy at birth in Shanghai, Beijing, Tianjin, and Hangzhou exceeded 80 years in 2010.

energy consumption will reach approximately 25%. After 2–3 five-year plan periods, China will strive to achieve a peak in its carbon emissions by 2020–2025. By 2030, emissions will begin to reduce to 2005 levels.

Bitter sacrifice strengthens bold resolve Which dares to make sun and moon shine in new skies.[6]

In 10 year's time, once China has created a prosperous society, what new development goals will be in place? What beautiful society will China embody after 20 years? By 2030, China will become a society of common prosperity created by the combined efforts of its vast population. This ideal of building an ambitious and beautiful society is both abstract and specific. Its implications and objectives are as follows:

1. It will be a society of common development shared by its people. The regional boundaries that have been in place for thousands of years, the rural/urban differences, and the gap between the rich and the poor will slowly disappear. The people will become the masters of the country. They will promote the development process and make concerted efforts to create material and spiritual wealth and to share the fruits of their development.
2. China will be a learning society. Education, information, and knowledge will become a daily necessity and the most important wealth of the people. All people will learn, at any time, and throughout their lives. Education will be the foundation of all, via a learning government, political parties, enterprises, communities, and families.
3. China will be a healthy society and a fitness-for-all society. China's people will enjoy long lives, and become healthier and happier. They will enjoy a lifestyle featuring health and good manners, with a lowering of all health risks and a reduction in chronic diseases. All of China's people will participate in daily physical exercise.
4. China's society will be characterized as having a high level of ecological civilization[7] and as being resource-efficient, environmentally friendly,[8] and climate-adaptive. In addition, it will be a society with a low risk of disasters, and harmony and common growth between man and nature.
5. China will be an innovative and knowledge-based society; the driving force behind both social and economic development.

---

[6] Mao Zedong, poem "Coming to Shaoshan", 1959.

[7] The report to the 16th Party congress points out that "The capability of sustainable development will be steadily enhanced. The ecological environment will be improved. The efficiency of using resources will be increased significantly. We will enhance harmony between man and nature to push the whole society onto a path to civilized development featuring the growth of production, an affluent life and a sound ecosystem" (Jiang Zemin 2005).

[8] An environmentally friendly society refers to a society of harmonious development between man and nature. Its purpose is to ensure favorable behavior toward the environment and to build a social system with the harmonious development of economy and society (see Ma Kai 2006).

6. China will be a society with a high level of political civilization. Its more than one billion people will become the masters of their country, with extensive political, economic, social, cultural, and democratic rights (in different forms) for all strata of society. Government at all levels will improve their policy-making, organization, mobilization, performance, and ability to adapt.
7. China will be a society with a high level of spiritual civilization.[9] The culture of the Chinese nation will flourish further and the use of soft power by the state will be further enhanced. There will be social conventions where everyone is responsible for safeguarding, creating, and maintaining harmony. China will become the largest society with the most advanced civilization, social ethics, and harmony.

"World of Great Harmony"

What is a world of great harmony? We hold that the most important tasks for China are to eliminate China's three boundaries and gaps. These are the boundaries and gaps between man and man, among different countries, and between man and nature. First, the three major centrisms must be broken down and communism promoted. This entails eliminating the elite centrism and the rich centrism with regard to people-to-people relationships. Instead, people-centrism and common prosperity must be encouraged. To follow, the North-centrism must be eliminated, as should the power politics centrism with regard to country-to-country relationships, and instead we need to advocate fairness, equality, and common prosperity. Finally, the notion of man conquering nature and the supremacy of development need to be eliminated, and instead we should advocate harmony, shared growth, and prosperity between man and nature.

By 2030, all of humanity will enter an exceptional era, which occurs only once every 1000 years, and will herald the advent of great harmony, a once in a millennium occurrence, during which we will all bear witness to great change. The events leading to 2030 will be represented in the following four trends, which are interrelated and mutually influencing:

1. **A trend of great development**. This refers largely to the development of the South, which will become the driving force behind the third golden age of development. The third golden age for the South cannot compare with the previous two golden ages of development. The golden age will be on a much larger scale because the South has such a large number of member countries (nearly 200), a vast population (six billion), rapid development (much faster than the North),

---

[9] As early as 1982, the report to the 12th National Party Congress set the objective of achieving a civilization with a high level of socialist spiritualism (Hu Yaobang 1982; see Central Documentation Office 1986).

and a strong commitment to economic globalization and integration. Urbanization will be accelerated, giving rise to the largest migration from rural areas to cities the world has ever seen. The whole world will enter an active period of innovation, and there will be an intense period of global development in the areas of science, technology and knowledge. The world will march toward common development and common progress.

2. **A trend of great convergence.** The world will enter a level of high human development, as the South will begin its period of economic takeoff, accelerating to catch up with the North. The levels of economic development of the South and the North will progress toward a great convergence, reducing the significant divergence of the past two centuries. The per capita GDP of the South will equal 33% of the North. Its level of human development will continue to move closer to that of developed countries. The absolute poverty of the past two centuries will essentially be eliminated, and the world will march toward common prosperity and common wealth.[10]

3. **A trend of reversibility.** The South–north pattern will be reversed, with the South to dominate the world economy, trade, and investment, ending two centuries of domination by the North. The ratio of the South and North economies will become 30:70 instead of 50:50. The South–north trade ratio will change from the current 40:60 to 70:30. The South will become the main recipient and exporter of external investments. The world's totals of the main economic indicators and the South's population percentage will converge. The world will become a sphere of greater equality.

4. **A trend of great changes.** Great changes will occur within the global economic development mode, and the economic, employment, and energy structures. The whole world will embrace a green energy revolution. Global governance mechanisms and structures will undergo significant changes too, with the South to become a main player and take greater roles, thus, enabling greater equality in the development of the world. The world will become more just and rational.

What is humanity's perfect ideal for the twenty-first century? We hold that the world, as a whole, will be a community of interests, a community of destiny, and a community of development. It is, therefore, necessary to jointly create a peaceful world, a harmonious world, a world of common prosperity, and a green world.

By 2030, China will become a dominant world power; what role will it play? Chinese leaders have answered by declaring that China, as a rising star, will not become conceited or complacent, and it will never invade others.[11] China will not

---

[10] The international absolute poverty line is less than 1.25 US dollars per person per day as defined by the World Bank. We estimate that the poverty occurrence rate in developing countries will drop from 27 % in 2005 to less than 5 % by 2030.

[11] In 1960, Mao Zedong said in his reply to Montgomery "China does not have a god, what it has is a Jade Emperor. Fifty years from now the Jade Emperor will still be reigning over 9.6 million square kilometers. We would be aggressors if we occupied an inch of land belonging to others" (Mao Zedong 1999a).

impose its ideology on others, it will not indulge in 'great-nation chauvinism',[12] and it will never seek hegemony.[13]

China is both the most populous country in the world and the biggest stakeholder of common interests. It is our true consideration, choice, and commitment to join the world and "share weal and woe" with all its inhabitants. We wish to work with the people of the world and to make concerted efforts to strive for common enrichment and prosperity, and to love our global homeland.

More than 50 years ago, Mao Zedong revealed China's intention to humanity when he said, "It [China] ought to make a greater contribution to humanity" by the year 2001.[14] In 1978, Deng Xiaoping went further to say China should make a greater contribution to the third world.[15] In 2007, Hu Jintao again said that China should make greater contributions to human civilization.[16] We hold that the twenty-first century is the century in which China will make huge contributions to human development.

What are these significant contributions? China's role and position in the world arena enables China to be an advocate for a "world of great harmony," an active participant and builder of a "world of great harmony," and the biggest contributor to a "world of great harmony."

China will become the biggest engine of growth of the world. China will become the world's biggest market, with increasingly strong positive externalities and a positive spillover effect. It will make increasingly significant contributions to the market,[17] trade,[18] employment, and investment.[19]

---

[12] In 1956, Mao Zedong said, "However, we should be modest – not only now, but 45 years hence and indeed always. In international relations the Chinese people should rid themselves of great-nation chauvinism resolutely, thoroughly, wholly and completely" (Mao Zedong 1999b).

[13] In 1987, Deng Xiaoping said "Should China become arrogant, however, act like an overlord and give orders to the world, it would no longer be considered a Third World country" (Deng Xiaoping 1984).

[14] In 1956, Mao Zedong in his "In Commemoration of Dr. Sun Yat-sen" said "It is only 45 years since the Revolution of 1911, but the face of China has entirely changed. In another 45 years, that is, by the year 2001, at the beginning of the twenty-first century, China will have undergone an even greater change. It will have become a powerful industrial socialist country. And that is as it should be. China is a land with an area of 9,600,000 km^2 and a population of 600 million, and it ought to make a greater contribution to humanity" (Mao Zedong 1999b).

[15] In 1957, Deng Xiaoping said: "At present, we are still a relatively poor nation. It is impossible for us to undertake many international proletarian obligations, so our contributions remain small. However, once we have accomplished the four modernizations and the national economy has expanded, our contributions to mankind, and especially to the Third World, will be greater" (Deng Xiaoping 1984).

[16] Hu Jintao said "When the goal of building a moderately prosperous society in all respects is attained by 2020, China, … will be still more open and friendly to the outside world and make greater contributions to human civilization." (Hu Jintao 2007; see Central Documentation Office 2009).

[17] China's average contribution was 14.6% in 2001–2009 to become the No. 1contributor to economic growth.

[18] According to statistics from UNTDC, China's percentage in goods import trade in the world rose from 4.4% to 8% for 2002–2009 and its percentage in the world's service import trade rose from 2.9 to 4.9%.

[19] In 2002–2009, the average annual contribution to global FDI inflow reached 3% and outflow, 5.5%.

China will become the largest development aid contributor. According to Deng Xiaoping's concept of "making greater contributions to the third world,"[20] China has formulated a new foreign aid program based on China's existing scheme.[21] This program requires "three steps." The first step is to bring the proportion of foreign aid in GDP to 0.3% by 2015; the second step is to increase it to 0.5% by 2020; the third step is to raise it to 1% or above by 2030. This will actively encourage other world powers, high-income countries, and emerging economies to increase the proportion of development aid in their GDPs and to expand the global aid program. It will also push the United Nations and other international organizations to formulate a millennium development goal (MDG) for 2015–2030. The targets of China's foreign aid program are fundamentally different from those of the Marshall Plan.[22] China mainly aids the least developed and developing countries, benefiting those countries in the South that are home to 80% of the world's population. As the biggest developing country, China has actively promoted South-South cooperation, trade and investment liberalization, and fair and even development between the South and the North.

China will become a leader in the worldwide process of great change. China is resolutely opposed to hegemony and power politics, and persists in the principle of equality for all countries, big or small, strong or weak, and rich or poor. China respects the rights of people of all countries in their free choice of the road they travel toward development (Hu 2007), and actively promotes fairer and more just international economic and political orders. China will make positive contributions

---

[20] Deng Xiaoping said, "once we have accomplished the four modernizations and the national economy has expanded, our contributions to mankind, and especially to the Third World, will be greater" (Deng Xiaoping 1984).

[21] China's foreign aid is made up of three categories: free aid, interest-free loans, and preferential loans. There are mainly eight forms of aid: complete plants, general materials, technical cooperation, cooperation in human resources development, medical teams, emergency humanitarian aid, volunteers, and debt reduction and exemption. According to the whitepaper on China's foreign aid, China has provided aid of 256.29 billion yuan, including 106.2 billion yuan free aid, 76.54 billion yuan interest-free loans, and 73.55 billion yuan of preferential loans, accounting for 41.4, 29.9 and 28.3%, respectively, in total foreign aid. China's foreign aid funds experienced rapid growth, with its average growth for 2004–2009 being 29.4%. By the end of 2009, China had helped developing countries build more than 2,000 complete plants associated closely with the livelihood and production of local peoples, covering industry, agriculture, culture and education, health, telecommunications, power, energy, and transportation. By the end of 2009, China had held more than 4,000 training classes for developing countries, training more than 120,000 people, including interns, management, and technical personnel and officials. By the end of 2009, China had sent more than 21,000 doctors, who treated more than 260 million people in recipient countries. By the end of 2009, China had signed debt-writing off protocols with 50 countries in Africa, Asia, Latin America, the Caribbean, and Oceania, writing off 380 debts, amounting to 25.58 billion yuan (equal to 17% of the total aid loans). State Council Information Office, "White Paper: China's Foreign Aid", April 21, 2011.

[22] The Marshall Plan, also known as the European Recovery Program stated that the United States was to provide economic aid to Western European countries that suffered in World War II and help them with their reconstruction. The plan ran from July 1947, and lasted for four fiscal years. Western European countries accepted a total of US$13 billion in aid, covering finance, technology and equipment.

to protecting the global environment, tackling global climate change, conserving
energy, reducing emissions, and promoting a green industrial revolution.

> Peace would then reign over the world,
>   the same warmth and cold throughout the globe (Mao Zedong 2003).

In October 1935, Mao Zedong arrived in the northern Shaanxi revolutionary
base. This period in history represents the most challenging period of China's revolution and the eve of the outbreak of World War II. However, Mao Zedong boldly
looked forward to a "peaceful world" that shares "the same warmth and cold."

In February, Deng Xiaoping positioned himself as a world citizen when he said
"I feel honored to become a world citizen in the capacity of a member of the Chinese
nation." He also stated, "China will work together with the rest of the world to promote human progress."[23] At that time, China had just begun its reform and opening
up. Its per capita GNP sat at the bottom of the world rankings. China was home to
the world's largest population living in absolute poverty. These circumstances
prompted Deng Xiaoping to promise to work for the just cause of human progress
in his capacity as a world citizen, and by embracing globalism.

By looking back through history and taking note of our historical responsibilities, we are more confident today in pursuing a world of great harmony. Thus, we
have arrived at the following consensus.[24]

1. **Common interests and common destiny.** We are aware of the many differences
   between countries; some countries are big and some are small, while others are
   rich and some are poor. Despite this, economic globalization and regional integration have enabled humanity to share common interests and a common destiny
   for the first time in history.
2. **Common challenges and cooperation.** We are aware that many challenges and
   developmental problems exist. However, these challenges are interrelated and
   mutually influencing, and will enable humanity to unite for the first time in
   history.
3. **Common prosperity and common wealth.** We are aware that countries are at
   different stages of development, with different development goals. However, a
   common destiny and common challenges have enabled humanity for the first
   time to jointly pursue common prosperity and common wealth. This requires that
   we aid developing countries and "send coal in snowy weather." Thus, we can
   help them to grow prosperous and wealthy.

"The world is beautiful but also not beautiful. There are good as well as bad
things in the world. It has been so since ancient times and will be so in 10,000 years"
(Mao Zedong 1999c). This will be true for China in 2030, and the rest of the world.
The world in 2030 will not be an ideal world. However, 2030 will not represent

---

[23] This is a foreword written by Deng Xiaoping on February 14, 1981 for the book *Speeches and
writings: Deng Xiaoping*, published by Pergamon Press Ltd (Central Documentation Office
2004).

[24] Jeffrey D. Sachs also holds that global cooperation will occur in the twenty-first century and that
competitive mindset regarding markets, power, and resources will ultimately be cast into history
(Sachs 2010).

the "end of history" either. The world in 2030 will be filled with contradictions and challenges, setbacks and conflicts. The global ecological crisis will not be fully resolved. Resource and energy shortages will become even more acute. An aging population will present further challenges. Local conflicts will be frequent, too. However, a new and better world will arrive before the expiration of our unjust world. We believe that the future generations will be wiser than we were, and that they will have many challenges and much work to do. Nevertheless, their prospects are bright too.

Humanity's Right Way

We have not tried to conceal the fact that we are optimists. This book has presented a glorious picture of China, and the world as a whole, for 2030.

We have done so because we have faith in the people, that they are the real motive force of history. They are the real heroes. When the more than one billion Chinese people (who are pursuing peace, happiness, and a better life) and the eight billion people of the world have become the true heroes, their potential will be fully released and they will surely become an inexhaustible source to propel our world toward a more beautiful tomorrow.

While the road ahead might be hard, the future is bright.[25] While retrogression is possible, history is always moving forward. Failure is inevitable, but success will predominate. We cannot stop China achieving common prosperity, nor the world in its quest for great harmony—it is a surging tide that cannot be held.

In addition, we believe that the road that we are taking is the right road. The socialist road is a broad path toward common wealth. The global view of sharing weal and woe is the path toward great harmony for the eight billion people of the world. History has proved this point and the future will continue to prove it.

We believe that to stand with the majority of the Chinese people and people worldwide is to stand on the right side of history, and the just side of history. We believe that the South (with 75% of the world's population) will become the first and foremost engine of human development and modernization in the twenty-first century.[26] The "South Wind," with the majority of developing countries, will overwhelm the "North Wind," representing a small number of developed countries.[27]

---

[25] Mao Zedong once said "But as we have often said, while the road ahead is tortuous, the future is bright" (Mao Zedong 1999d).

[26] This is reiterated by Harvard history and economics professor David S. Landes, who said that for thousands of years, Europe (Western) has been the first to seek development and modernization (see Landes 2001).

[27] Here, we refer to Mao Zedong's "East Wind Overwhelms the West Wind". On November 18, 1957, Mao Zedong said at the Conference of Communist Parties and Worker's parties "Now I feel that the international situation is at a new turning point. There are two gusts of winds, east wind and west wind. A Chinese idiom says: it is either east wind overwhelming the west wind or the west wind overwhelming the east wind. I think the characters of the current situation are east wind whelming the west wind. That is, the socialist forces have an overwhelming advantage over the imperialist forces." *Collected Works of Mao Zedong*, Vol. VII, p. 321, Beijing, People's publishing House.

We believe that only by representing the interests of the overwhelming majority of the Chinese people and people worldwide, is it possible to embark on a course that is both optimistic and victorious.

In 1956, Mao Zedong said, "The future of China is to build socialism. It will take 50–100 years to make China a strong and prosperous country. Now there is no force obstructing China's development" (Mao Zedong 1999e). Thus, as stated by Hu Jintao at a rally marking the 90th anniversary of the founding of the Communist Party of China, "So long as we do not waver, do not slack off and do not cause troubles again and again, are not afraid of any risks and do not feel dizzy by any interference (Hu Jintao 2011), there will be no force obstructing China's development" (Mao Zedong 1999e).

In December 1964, Mao Zedong set an ambitious goal: to create a modern and strong socialist country within a brief historical period. This produced many doubters, both in China and overseas. Mao Zedong retorted, "Can't we achieve it? Is it bragging and mutter high-sounding words? No. We can achieve it. It is neither bragging nor muttering high-sounding words. You will know it when you look at our history. Why the oriental proletariat cannot achieve what western bourgeoisie can achieve?" (Mao Zedong 1999f)

At that time, the United States' GDP was 5.4 times that of China.[28] Although Mao Zedong was unaware of this, he had the ambition and the foresight. He shunned what has been termed in China 'crawlism' (crawling behind others in science, technological and economic terms) and was the first to consider leapfrog development. The facts speak for themselves, as 40–50 years on China has indeed pioneered its own development path and has realized leapfrog development, greatly narrowing the relative GDP gap with the United States. Before long will China will overtake the United States.

It took China just a number of decades to achieve what the United States achieved in more than 200 years. China has achieved what the United States could not in more than 200 years;[29] that is, a socialist society of common wealth, created by China's united population of more than one billion people. Now that China has achieved its dream, it will show the way for the South (Deng Xiaoping 1993), so that the eight billion people of the world can create and share a "world of great harmony."

---

[28] Source: Maddison (2010).

[29] As the most powerful and developed capitalist country, the United States, has not yet resolved various welfare issues. 1. Medical insurance. In 2009, 59 million people (20% of the population) were not covered by medical insurance (Centers for Disease Control and Prevention). A study report released by Harvard University in 2009 claimed that 44,800 died because they had no medical insurance. 2. Public security. The United States has some of the world's highest murder rates (greater than 5 deaths per 100,000 people) (UNODC, Homicide Statistics, Criminal Justice and Public Health Sources - Trends (2003–2008)); 3. Employment. The United States has the highest unemployment rate among developed countries, with a 2010 unemployment rate of 9.63% (www.bls.gov/bls/cpsaat2).

References

CPC Central Documentation Office (1986) Selected important documents since the 12th National Party Congress, vol 1. People's Publishing House, Beijing, p 26

CPC Central Documentation Office (2004) Chronicle of Deng Xiaoping (1975–1997), vol II. Central Documentation Press, Beijing, pp 713–714

CPC Central Documentation Office (2009) Selected important documents since the 17th National Party Congress, vol 1. People's Publishing House, Beijing, p 16

Deng Xiaoping (1984) Realize the four modernizations and never seek hegemony, May 7, 1978. In: Selected works of Deng Xiaoping. People's Publishing House, Beijing, p 112

Deng Xiaoping (1993) Adopt a clear-cut stand against bourgeois liberalization, December 30, 1986. In: Selected works of Deng Xiaoping, vol 3. People's Publishing House, Beijing, pp 195–196

Hu Yaobang (1982) Break new ground in socialist modernization. Report to the 12th National Party Congress, 1 Sept 1982

Hu Jintao (2007) Hold high the great banner of socialism with Chinese characteristics and strive for new victories in building a moderately prosperous society in all respects. Report to the 17th national congress of the communist party of China, 15 Oct 2007

Hu Jintao (2011) Speech at the rally marking the 90th anniversary of the founding of the communist party of China, Xinhua, Beijing, 1 July

Jiang Zemin (2005) Build a complete well-off Society and open new ground in the cause of socialism with Chinese characteristics. Held in CPC Central Research Office, Selected important documents since the 16th National Party Congress, vol 1. Central documentation Press, Beijing, p 14

Landes D (2001) The wealth and poverty of nations, Chinese edn. Xinhua Publishing House, Beijing, p 6

Ma Kai (ed) (2006) Guide to reading the outline program of the 11th five-year plan for national economic and social development of the People's Republic of China. Beijing Science and Technology Press, p 515

Maddison A (2010) Statistics on world population, GDP and Per Capita GDP, 1–2008 AD. http://www.ggdc.net/MADDISON/oriindex.htm

Mao Zedong (1991) On coalition government, April 24, 1945. In: Selected works of Mao Zedong, vol 3. People's Publishing House, Beijing, p 1,031

Mao Zedong (1996) Train and bring up successors to the cause of proletarian revolution, June 16, 1964. In: Manuscripts of Mao Zedong since the founding of the People's republic of china, vol 11. Central Documentation Press, Beijing, p 85

Mao Zedong (1999a) Talks with Montgomery, May 27, 1960. In: Collected works of Mao Zedong, vol 8. People's Publishing House, Beijing, p 189

Mao Zedong (1999b) In commemoration of Dr. Sun Yat-sen, November 12, 1956. In: Collected works of Mao Zedong, vol 7. People's Publishing House, Beijing, pp 156–157

Mao Zedong (1999c) Do not blindly believe that everything is good in a socialist country, June 28, 1956. In: Collected works of Mao Zedong, vol VII. People's Publishing House, Beijing, p 69

Mao Zedong (1999d) On ten major relationships, April 25, 1956. In: Collected works of Mao Zedong, vol VII. People's Publishing House, Beijing, p 44

Mao Zedong (1999e) Draw on historical lessons and oppose great nation Chauvinism, September 24, 1956. In: Collected works of Mao Zedong. People's Publishing House, Beijing, p 124

Mao Zedong (1999f) Build China into a modern and strong socialist country, December 13, 1964. In: Collected works of Mao Zedong, vol VIII. People's Publishing House, Beijing, p 341

Mao Zedong (2003) Poem "Kunlun – to the tune of Nien Nu Jiao", Oct 1935. In CPC Central Documentation Office, Collection of Mao Zedong's poems. Central Documentation Press, Beijing, p 52

Sachs JD (2010) Common wealth economics for a crowded planet, Chinese edn., CITIC Publishing House, Beijing, p 3

Lightning Source UK Ltd.
Milton Keynes UK
UKHW02f0625310718

326547UK00004B/100/P